KEEN
for Learning

Why Some Kids Don't Succeed in the Classroom—and

What We Can Do About It

by Edmond J. Dixon, PhD

Published by Wintertickle **PRESS**
92 Caplan Avenue, Suite 155, Barrie, ON, L4N 7Z3
www.TeachEasy.net
www.WinterticklePress.com
www.WinterticklePress.co.uk

Printed and bound in Canada
ISBN 1894813-52-9

www.KeenForLearning.org

For my Mom and Dad...

Acknowledgements

It's hard to know where to start, when thousands of people have supported your work, but I would like to thank all of those students and teachers who have been part of this journey. A few educators have gone above and beyond in their support for my work and I would like to acknowledge Brian Jones, Alyson McLelland, Catarina Burisch, Candice Higgs, Heather Groves, Carl Riley, Sheila Chichelnik, and Mary-Ann Cheung for their belief in the power of this approach.

Our small band of instructors and office support staff made up of Katie Pitt, Kathryn Coates, Gary Leech, Rosemary Rock-Vincent, and Julie Ditta are to be thanked for their professionalism and flexibility. Grant D'Eall has provided support and advice at many points on this journey and Rob Chung has been our KEEN instructor extraordinaire, never ceasing to find new ways to improve our work; I am proud to call both of them colleagues and friends.

The theoretical basis underlying KEEN Differentiated Learning was developed during my research at the University of Toronto. I owe a debt of gratitude to the Ontario Institute for Studies in Education and to Dr. Linda Cameron, Dr. David Booth, and Dr. Larry Swartz for helping me navigate the uncertain seas of PhD research and always encouraging me to set high standards in my work.

I am awed by the work of Catherine A. Fish, my copy editor, as well as that of my editor/publisher at WintertticklePress,

Heather Down. They did amazing things with short timelines!

Finally, thanks to my family: my son Andrew, who taught with us early on, my other son; Stephen, who drove many kilometers so that I could sit next to him and write (and not escape before the task was done!); and my wife, Joanne, who has endured much so that I could embark on this quest to improve learning for kids in other people's families. I am blessed to have the love and support of those closest to me.

About Notes & References

This book is designed to introduce busy educators to a new and exciting way of engaging and teaching students. Much of the approach is grounded in research and supported by educational writers. Where that is so, a reference note has been made. I have always found, however, that when reading to understand it can be distracting to do so with a text filled with references and footnotes. While useful for a researcher, they can diminish the experience for the practicing teacher, administrator, or member of the general population. So I have chosen not to put notes in the text; rather, all of the notes that support my writing can be found at the back of the book with a reference to the quote and page they support. If you read something interesting that you want to read more about, just flip to the back!

Table of Contents

PART I

THE

Challenges

WE

FACE

Chad

"Let's face it Mr. Dixon: I'm stupid—You know it, I know it, and my parents know it."

I looked at the 14-year-old across from me. For a brief moment his eyes glistened, daring me to refute him. His happy-go-lucky demeanor had vanished; in its place, he radiated a sense of shame, fear, and hopelessness that enveloped me as well. It only lasted a brief moment and then Chad returned to his adolescent insouciance and world-weary mask that teenagers use to keep adults at bay. He leaned back in his chair and stared at the assignment that he had been sent down to the office to complete.

It wasn't supposed to go like this. There was only one week left before Chad "graduated" into high school, yet we continued to have numerous principal-bad boy conversations where I cajoled him into getting the minimum done so he could return to class. The general perception of Chad was that he was a "slacker" who would not amount to much. Everything about his approach to school and learning was defined by a lack of interest and avoidance. I saw him differently: popular with his peers and an excellent skateboarder with a keen sense of humour, I enjoyed talking to him and delighted in his inquiring mind and sharp observations on human nature. It was in practical situations—like the school play—that he really shone. I had directed Chad in a school play earlier in the year and had witnessed his excellent sense of timing, ability to memorize numerous lines, and diligent work backstage. He displayed dedication and seriousness.

"You have such potential—why can't you put the same effort into class?" I asked him again.

It was this question that prompted his declaration of stupidity. The fierceness of it stunned me. I had worked 25 years with young people as a teacher and principal and knew this was not an act. He seemed just as surprised by what had happened as I, as if he had revealed a deeply buried secret when his mask of indifference had slipped.

"You're not stupid," I said weakly. I knew as the words left my mouth that they were inadequate—even sacrilegious—in that moment. We had moved into a more profound territory and so, despite my usual irredeemable tendency to fill the air with words, I remained quiet. He did not move. A tear slowly made its way down his cheek.

After he left I stared out the window of my office for a long time. The recess bell rang as I watched the yard fill with excited children. Four boys in kindergarten crouched intently gazing at the ground, conferencing about what they were looking at. One of them poked at it with a stick and the others smiled broadly and started talking and gesturing excitedly. They had discovered something new and were enthralled. Did *they* believe they were stupid? I didn't think so. When I observed them in class they appeared to be passionate about learning anything and everything they could, particularly if they could engage it with their whole being. What would happen between now and a time 10 years later when, if statistics were accurate, one of those children would drop out of school? Chad seemed well on his way to that destination.

The bell rang to signal the end of recess and students lined up to enter the building. The body language of the older students began to transform, appearing less at ease. They looked resigned as teachers called them in as if they were preparing to enter a decompression chamber. I knew that if I walked into a classroom a few minutes later—particularly of older kids—there would be less of the passion and excitement I witnessed at recess.

Why?

The classroom was designed for learning and human growth; it should be the most exciting place in the school. If there are such places, I have seen it only infrequently. Most of the joy I experienced in school both as a student and as a teacher had taken place outside of the classroom with activities that appeared tangential to classroom work. Ironically, I was a "winner" in the system who found it so meaningful that I chose to remain in school and educate others. But my time as a principal troubled me because I discovered that Chad was not an anomaly: He represented many others who were underachieving and found school meaningless—even if they were getting good grades. But the ones who were excelling would probably not be dropping out, their lives filled with many more opportunities than Chad's. Why was that? And how likely was it that they felt as stupid as Chad did?

I didn't know what to think as these questions persisted in my mind. I knew one thing, however: A school experience that leaves a student with the profound belief that he is stupid is not a school experience likely to serve him well in life. Success in achieving one's goals in life largely depends on two things: a sense of passion for those goals and the confidence and efficacy to achieve them. What would it take to make classrooms an environment where every student received those things?

That is what this book is about. It is the fruit of 3 years of intensive theory and practice that came as a result of my decision, after 25 years in education, to leave my position as a school principal in the hope of finding better ways to help kids like Chad. The theoretical aspect involved my doctoral research at the University of Toronto, where I was able to extensively study recent educational and scientific research on how the brain learns. At the same time, a group of like-minded educators and I were able to work with more than 50,000 students, teachers, and administrators to develop and field test what now makes up the KEEN Differentiated Learning. This dual approach proved ideal for developing a model of experiential learning that is both supported by research and works in the classroom. The voices and anecdotes you'll find throughout the following chapters are those of the adults and children who experienced and came to believe in the power of KEEN Learning.

As a result of these diverse perspectives, this book also has a rather unique mission. It is designed to provide a broad overview of the challenges we face as a society in educating our children for the future, but it is also intended to be a practical tool that helps teachers generate student engagement and cognition. To get there, however, the reader must consider a new perspective based on brain science that changes classroom practice for the better. Those who work in the classroom must value the powers of the body and our genetic inheritance as much as we value the intellect. If we are willing to do this then, paradoxically, we can gain the ability to strengthen the powers of the intellect in those students who struggle most in school.

The book is divided into three sections in an effort to address the different aspects of its mission, and I encourage readers to explore every chapter before deciding on its merits or even applying its principles. If you are a practicing teacher, your first inclination might be to jump to the last section on KEEN strategies and get right into the nitty-gritty. However, your efforts will not reach their potential unless you understand *why* and *how* it works. Likewise, if you work outside the classroom (administrator, consultant, journalist, researcher, parent) but are concerned with what goes on inside, the first chapters might resonate strongly, but the specific strategies may be of less initial interest. Here, too, I encourage you to consider them—they offer practical solutions to the problems highlighted in earlier sections, and it is paramount for all readers to understand the big picture. Approaching the book this way puts you in the best position to benefit from it and to play your part in helping improve the lives of millions of young people.

CHAPTER 1
Classroom Learning and Life

"Education is not a preparation for life; education is life itself."
—John Dewey

What's Up with the Classroom?

When you think about it, school is a funny place. We suspend the normal activities of life and place children in an artificial learning environment (a classroom) to learn what they'll need to be successful in society later on. Schools contain classrooms in which heterogeneous groups of children are placed together and taught "subjects." The school identifies certain things as important to learn (parallelograms) and others as not very important (making a variety of funny faces), proceeding to tell students how successful they are based on whether they can demonstrate that they have learned the important things.

As artificial as it is, the classroom model is prevalent in North American society. Look at almost any learning situation today for any age group: Whether it's in elementary or secondary school, college or university, corporate training, language instruction, driver's training, or hobby classes, it is predominately the preferred way for groups to learn. One of the reasons that it's so ubiquitous in our millennium, despite the new learning opportunities available to individuals through the media and the Internet, is that most adults experienced classrooms as the place for learning as children. It is so familiar that each of us feels that, in a sense, we understand the classroom because we have all experienced it.

It also has extremely powerful effects: Students who are successful in their first 10 years in the classroom environment tend to accumulate many years of schooling after and are, on the whole, statistically wealthier, happier, and more successful in setting and achieving life goals than those who don't—they even live longer! The same is true for countries. Those who have the most well-developed school systems—almost all based on classrooms—are at the top of the list for per capita income, life expectancy, and quality of life indicators. This has been a discernable trend for the last century. Governments have recognized this by increasing spending on education in the last few decades and by paying extremely close attention to dropout rates, with the stated aim of having every student well educated and, most famously in the United States, "no child left behind."

What many don't realize is that the belief that every child should learn in the classroom is a truly radical idea. For most of education in the last 100 years, children have been left behind, flunked out, or allowed not to have success and that was acceptable. School was a place to rank and sort students by ability and effort. The common approach was "You can lead a horse to water but you can't make him drink." Teachers were charged with presenting material in a structured and logical way and assessing students' ability to learn that material. After World War II, the overall graduation rate was between 65% and 70%. From 1950 to 1970, it ranged from 73% to 80% and is presently anywhere between 75% and 85% depending on how it is tabulated. So what happened to those students who did not graduate? They went into the workforce or into specialized vocational training. Many who did so had very successful outcomes, earning a good living and becoming valuable members of their communities and contributing to society.

Those who leave school in North America no longer have the opportunities afforded to previous generations. Today's children must not only stay in school but must also prepare themselves for a lifetime of learning that will take place in postsecondary education, in the workplace, and beyond. And that means they will spend a lot of time in classrooms.

The Fear of Classroom Learning and Its Consequences

So what changes have been made to make sure that this new cohort of students—those who might have left school in previous generations—has success in the classroom? As vital as it is that schools educate every child, we have found it challenging to educate students who struggle in the classroom and because of this we have millions who leave our school system like Chad, believing they are stupid when it comes to classroom learning. The consequences of this are tragic.

For those still in school, their level of engagement is reduced dramatically and their effort at learning decreases progressively with each year they stay in school. I spent a number of years at an inner-city high school and it was obvious which students arrived already finished with learning; they had little self-confidence on academic tasks, were not resilient when they encountered difficulties, and were fearful about taking risks in the classroom, preferring to put as little effort as possible into activities. They often masked their fear of learning with bravado, sarcasm, classroom disruption, or absence from class. But when one got to know them, the fear and loathing that Chad had revealed to me became readily apparent. They *wanted* to learn, but felt it was beyond them. And for the fragile ego that accompanies one in the high school years, this was too much to bear. So they flunked out and left.

For those who leave school with the belief that they cannot learn in that environment, it can negatively colour the way they approach formal learning for the rest of their lives. Because school is such a seminal and powerful experience, failure in that context will cause them to consciously avoid future situations in which they have to be in a classroom or demonstrate their ability to learn in a structured learning situation. They may end up avoiding training courses or other such opportunities necessary to help them achieve their goals. If they do find themselves in these settings, they disengage emotionally to avoid the pain of failure, refraining from asking questions, participating in discussions, seeking extra help, or anything else exposing their "stupidity" to others. It is tragic to think how much this attitude contributes to the constriction of opportunity for individuals, not to mention the loss society suffers when its members do not reach the highest levels of potential that learning provides.

To be sure, there are a few who become "self-teachers" and pursue their own interests and develop a love of learning. Some of the most fascinating and erudite people I know maintained a passion for education despite what they experienced in school; their natural stubbornness and contrarian natures gave them an understanding like that of Mark Twain who quipped, "I never let schooling interfere with my education." A surprising number of entrepreneurs are of this ilk.

The distrust that many of them share about their school experience is well represented by this entrepreneur:

> Growing up almost every teacher I had discouraged me from being myself. They said I needed to talk less, do as I am told...just couldn't handle teachers. Teachers definitely could not handle me. I believed in myself too much. I would rarely care about what the teachers told me about success. This does not mean I blatantly disrespected teachers. I would do my work and move on...The biggest lesson that school does not teach student is how the world "actually" works."

12

This attitude vis-à-vis learning does contribute to entrepreneurial success but can eventually become a handicap. A consultant whose role is to help small business people take their enterprises to the next level once confided to me that he was very frustrated in trying to help many of his clients because their own mindset was the only thing preventing them from achieving greater success. Specifically, he attributed this to their refusal to believe they could learn anything important that they hadn't experienced themselves. This led them to disregard sage advice, micromanage their enterprises, and refuse to delegate. Is it possible that this self-defeating refusal to learn from others could have its roots in their childhood school experience where their failures in the classroom made them determined to prove to everyone they weren't failures as people? At the same time, this made them impossible to teach—even the things they knew they needed to learn. Even when success follows, a sense of failure in the classroom can restrict individuals and deprive society of their full contributions.

Better Classroom Experience for Strugggling Students

What if the classroom became a place where every child could not only learn but also believe in their capability to learn? A place where all students were passionate and engaged and working at their fullest capacity? What differences would that make in the lives of individuals, families, and indeed our social fabric? How much better would we be prepared to face the challenges of a post-industrial society that requires constant and consistent learning and innovation to maintain our standard of living, give its members meaningful roles, and pass on a better world to those who will come behind us?

We are at a moment in time where classroom learning is poised to undergo a process resulting in tremendous gains in effectiveness for a larger number of students. This book is designed to help jumpstart that process by synthesizing a number of recent influences which, when used together, hold great potential to supercharge learning in the classroom. Those influences are:

- The general overall acceptance of the idea that different people learn in different ways and that the classroom should accommodate their learning styles

- The latest brain science research that deepens our understanding of how the brain works and the best way to facilitate learning

- A new understanding of how simple activities, when used as teaching methods, can affect the brain in such a way that learning is triggered and is in congruence with the findings of brain science

- A distillation of advances in methods for teacher development that make improving classroom practice easier and more effective

When we understand these influences, it is possible to see a new approach that fuses student engagement with cognition to generate passion for learning and skill development. It is only through this approach that the fear of classroom learning afflicting so many students can be alleviated. The key to success in the classroom is helping each individual recover the joy that they experienced daily as a child learning about the world in which they lived. Indeed, that is the only way forward if we want to have learning in our schools and institutions develop its true potential for our era.

The contribution I hope to make in this book is to describe how this new approach can be embodied in a series of simple and effective classroom strategies that fit easily into daily school routines. They can be used across the curriculum and have been battle-tested with many students and teachers in the past few years. They are both inspirational and effective at helping teachers motivate and teach both at-risk students as well as those who already experience classroom success. Best of all, they bring a sense of joy and adventure to even the driest areas of the curriculum—for both teachers *and* students!

CHAPTER 2

A Littered Landscape

Mrs. Sedgway was taking up the morning's homework with her Grade 4 class, writing the answers on the board. As she turned to the class she noticed a 9-year-old boy slink in and sit down heavily at his desk. He was more than 45 minutes late—for the third time that week. Exasperated, she declared loudly, "Robert, you should have been here at 9 o'clock!" The boy looked up hopefully and said, "Why? What happened!?"

The Paradox of Learning

Imagine yourself walking down the hallway of an average school. If we saw quiet hallways, children in classrooms sitting at their desks reading, writing and doing assignments, most of us would take this as normal. If, when the bell rang, the children in the classrooms noisily and excitedly and went outside for recess, we would also view that as normal. And we would be right—that's normal for most schools. But what if I asked you to rate the level of each of the following as demonstrated by the students in both situations?

1. Passion
2. Engagement
3. Cognitive Intensity

Where would you find the greatest levels? In my many years of experience in schools as a student, teacher, parent, and administrator, I would observe the greatest levels of all three were more often found at recess and not in the classroom. It happens so often that we accept it as normal—but is it? I always wonder: *Why should this be so?*

Go to a school at recess; watch the students. Look at how seriously they spend their time playing, exploring, and discovering the thrill and heartbreak of relationships, how to navigate social groupings, and how to gain mastery in any number of things they're interested in. Yet go into a classroom after recess and you will notice quite a difference. The enthusiasm that was present in most of the students outside, appears present in far fewer students. We know statistically that millions of students in North American classrooms will not complete high school. These unengaged students may be disruptive, but if they are not, many just sit there like bumps on a log. How many parents have had the following conversation that I regularly had with my sons in their school years:

"What did you learn in school today?"

"Nothing."

Well, not exactly nothing; with persistent parental prying, it turned out that a lot of interesting things happened, often pertaining to social relationships, a new accomplishment, or challenges they faced that were real and important to them. But rarely did any of this have anything to do with what happened in class. Again, I wondered: *Why is this?*

You might easily respond that the classroom is work and recess is *play*, which is fun. Part of learning and maturing is developing the ability to work in such contexts so we can earn a living and be productive to society first and then take our recess—weekends, vacations, etc. But one of the paradoxes of studying the lives of those we hold up to kids as models— the great achievers in business, science, and politics—is that passion, engagement, and cognitive intensity were the catalysts for their achievements. Furthermore, many of them treat their work as play—it's fun for them. Looking at their lives from the outside, we may see long hours, failures, and disappointments and tedium that marked their journey toward achievement as anything but fun, but it was their drive based on passionate engagement and cognitive intensity that helped them weather the difficulties. Without them, they would never have accomplished as much as they did—all of the work would have had no meaning.

The paradox is that *the work of learning needs the joy of learning* if it is to have meaning and any long-lasting effect on those who experience it. As we shall see, the context of education in advanced societies has changed so radically in the past 20 years that it has changed all the rules. This has highlighted other paradoxes. Learning is recognized almost universally in our culture as valuable, yet our education system makes many people unhappy and dissatisfied. Students in a significant number of classrooms spend up to half of their day copying notes and information that has very little meaning to them from blackboards, "smart" boards, overheads, and books, only to have to regurgitate this information at a later time. When they go home, however, they immediately access many times more information on the Internet. This information has much more meaning to them and engages them—and often causes them to write more than they do in school. Children who will not spend 5 minutes on school assignments spend hours on video games.

Colleges, universities, and other institutes of "higher learning" to which every child is encouraged to aspire regularly have to deal with scandals resulting from "pretend" academic courses taken by their athletes, grade inflation, or student cheating. Inner-city youth idolize music and sports celebrities, and surveys consistently indicate that they believe they have a realistic chance of being like them and earning the lifestyle of those celebrities. They will spend hours practicing skills and routines, despite the fact that in reality, the chances of them achieving professional success is miniscule. Yet these same young people do not feel they have any chance of becoming professionals like doctors, lawyers, and engineers and put little effort toward those goals, even though statistically they have a much greater chance of doing so. "Good" schools are often judged to be those with a vibrant school culture where sports and other extra-curricular activities flourish and young people enthusiastically join in, yet classrooms, where the "real learning" is supposed to take place, can appear to be passionless places, where most students participate with an air of resignation, marking time and waiting for the bell. Then—and only then— do they come to life.

One could say that many of these paradoxes in classroom education have existed for a long time, perhaps since formal education began, and that from a realistic and practical viewpoint, classroom education has proved itself widely useful, necessary and is here to stay. I would agree with the importance and longevity of the classroom, but its shortcomings have now become acute—particularly for those students who most desperately need what the classroom offers: a way out of poverty and discrimination and a pathway to a better life. Tragically, it is these very students that it most often fails and for them that I have written this book. Let's look at who these students are and why the classroom is becoming less and less effective in helping them.

Those Who Are Not Succeeding

It is generally accepted that completing high school is a prerequisite for successful participation in our post-industrial society. Dropout rates range widely in North America, but they are highest in areas of poverty and among males. In the U.S., the rate for white students was 22% in 2003, compared with 28% for Asian students, 45% for African American students, and 47% for Hispanic students. Female students drop out at a lower rate than male students with 28% of females dropping out, compared with 45% of males. The gender gap is particularly large for minority students. In Canada the statistics are similar, where nearly 60% of dropouts are male—with even higher rates for minority students. The Toronto District School Board, Canada's largest school board, recently published a report finding the dropout rate among certain groups of minority students averaged nearly 40%. Dropouts of all varieties comprise 82% of the prison population in the U.S. and 74% in Canada.

We know that this problem does not begin in high school. These students are apparent to teachers at every stage of education. They are children who may have tolerated being in my school or classroom, and even may have gone through the motions of learning, but no lasting learning took place for them. They did not retain the information or many of the skills that were imparted and, most importantly, they did not become passionate about learning. This "school stuff" was not their thing. It might be endured, but not embraced. Ask any teacher and they will be able to tell you about such students, whose faces they can visualize many years later. It seems that the longer one teaches children, the greater this collection expands.

Compared to students who succeed, these children are:

- More disengaged in the classroom

- Require more disciplinary interventions from the teachers and principal
- Absent from school more often
- More likely to be in remedial and special education classes

They take up an inordinate amount of time and energy from the adults in the school and, ultimately, a teacher often heaves a sigh of relief when they "move on" to another class. Typically, most faculty in the school system *know* who the struggling students are. Yet, despite significant investments in educational time and resources, there has been slow progress in helping them succeed in the classroom and—by extension—in the school system.

Why Are They Not Succeeding?

The reason a quarter of the students in any classroom struggle has to do with the fact that classroom learning was never really designed to effectively educate these students. As indicated in Chapter 1, they often regularly left school in the past for vocational training, trades, and the general workforce. It was in these settings that their learning style—which required an experiential, kinesthetic, and practical orientation—was most effectively addressed. Today, those options are no longer available to them. Vocational training has mostly migrated to the community college level or independent fee-for service institutions. The trades are difficult to enter into, and immediate entry into the workforce restricts a 16-year-old to mostly low-paying employment in the service sector, and even those jobs are harder to find in recessionary times due to increased competition from older, more experienced workers. Not to mention the fact that this type of work rarely forms the basis for a successful career. Governments and educators have recognized this and in some jurisdictions require students to stay in school longer (e.g., Ontario law mandates that students stay in school until they are 18 years old).

Despite the great emphasis on keeping these students in school, the nature of their schooling has not substantially changed to accommodate them. Instead, their learning style is largely ignored in the classroom, despite research indicating they need differentiated learning. I believe there are some very specific reasons why this is happening, and they can be related to how we approach learning with these students. Yet much of the debate has focused on the students themselves, specifically what is "wrong" with them that—if fixed—could have them succeed. Let's reflect on some of the most commonly held perceptions:

It's an Ability Issue – *The kids aren't smart enough; they can't learn what they need to be taught. They just aren't cut out for school learning.* Do you know when we learn the most? Between the time we are born and 5 years of age, we learn the incredible complexities of eating by ourselves, regulating our bowels, walking, talking, and navigating our physical and social world. Compared to these challenges, learning how to spell correctly in Grade 2 should be a piece of cake. Every child who enters a kindergarten classroom has already demonstrated a tremendous ability to learn. As we shall see, context often defines ability. The question may well not be if they have the ability to learn, but rather, if the classroom structure provides all students with the right context in which to learn.

It's a Character Issue – *These kids are lazy, they don't want to work, want everything for free, etc.* Well, if in the midst of all of that complex learning they were doing before they entered school, they watched a bit of TV or internalized any of the mainstream media around them, they might be forgiven for believing the advertising promising them they could get something for nothing. But that's not really the point. All children are products of the culture in which they grow up. The fact is that if one observes these lazy students closely, one can almost always find areas into which they will put a great deal of effort and "work" very hard. It's just that these can more often be found on the soccer pitch or the video screen and not in the classroom.

It's the Family – *The school is not supported at home, parents don't value education, have not provided educational opportunities, don't set guidelines for homework and reasonable bedtimes, they are absent, the family unit is dysfunctional, etc.* No educator can deny the immense power of family support and encouragement for school achievement. Our job is much easier when these highlighted issues do not exist. And yet, how is it that millions of children are able to perform in the classroom despite one or more of these disadvantages? What motivated them to so? On average, children in school spend more waking time in class than with their families. I firmly believe that what happens there can mitigate the effects of troubled family life.

It's a Poverty/Racism Issue - *The deck is stacked against those in poverty and people of colour. School systems don't value or understand the cultural backgrounds of their children, and give economically disadvantaged children the same benefits it does to wealthier children.* These societal issues are both real and harmful to young people who experience them. Yet again, how does this explain those impoverished and minority students who have achieved in the classroom and pursued their dreams into adulthood, rising out of poverty and showing that the colour of their skin has nothing to do with their ability to achieve? As well, if one examines North American education, there has been a tremendous effort in the past half century to alleviate and accommodate the challenges presented by these problems with increased funding for impoverished areas, breakfast programs, family support groups, culturally sensitive curricula, etc. And yet the stubborn persistence of dropout rates shows that those efforts have still not resulted in wholesale success in the classroom—in fact, they sometimes have very little effect on classroom practice.

I am not discounting that these varying challenges just described are reality for children and teachers who find themselves together in the classroom. What's important to recognize is that student success in the classroom can still occur and what happens in that classroom has the potential for far more power than what happens outside of it. Why? Because it is a place where a new context can be created for kids. A *context* in which equity of opportunity is built into daily classroom learning. Those of us who have lived a bit know that most of success in life is context. When we are put in a situation that allows us to perform in the way that is most natural, interesting, and in tune with our abilities, then we perform successfully.

Human history shows that individuals can learn to overcome any obstacle if we have a strong enough *desire*. That desire is characterized by the passion, engagement, and cognitive intensity that allow us to gain the skills to meet the challenges necessary for success—and it can be fostered in the classroom. Indeed, teachers do it every day for millions of students in North America, but still not for a significant minority, despite the fact that their out-of-school lives have confirmed they have the ability to work hard and learn. So what is the problem with their learning in the classroom? To answer that question, we must frame it existentially.

The Search for Meaning

Beyond our basic biological needs for food, shelter, and physical safety, the search for meaning is paramount. Psychologists like Abraham Maslow to Victor Frankel have written eloquently about this. The power of religions and spiritual movements attest to the fact that as humans we are meaning-makers. In the classroom, meaning is no less important. How many times in our school careers did we hear a teacher say "You're going to need to know this!" as an attempt to attach meaning to what followed. Honestly, though, how many of us really believed that it had practical meaning to us when we heard it?

…Parallelograms?

…The date of the French Revolution?

…The importance of gerunds?

C'mon…

So why did we learn it? Because we found the significance in one of the following:

Intrinsic Motivation To Achievement
"If I don't know this I won't do well on the test and I like doing well on tests."

Desire to Please
"If I don't know this I won't do well on the test and my parents (teachers) won't be happy with me."

Desire To Avoid Perceived Negative Consequences
"If I don't know this I won't do well on the test I and…I might get grounded…OR…I might fail and not pass Grade 5…OR…I might fail and then not graduate…and have a TERRIBLE life…Ahhh!!"

We might smile at the neurosis evident in the last thought, but I can tell you from my years as an educator that certain students have this intense fear of failure. It's not often readily apparent because those students usually succeed in the classroom. As a matter of fact, I notice that a surprising number of them go on to become teachers!

There is another way that meaning can be attached, although for most classroom subjects it affects only a small minority of students. That is through **Internal Attraction and Enjoyment** and is best reflected this way:

"Those lines in the parallelogram are pretty cool looking— why is everything bent like that?"

Something about the topic has caught our fancy, ignited our imagination, and seemed fun to our minds. Students who find meaning in subject matter this way tend to learn deepest and most enthusiastically.

But what about children where there is no internal attraction, no desire to please, no intrinsic motivation to achieve, and no fear of consequences? Where in the classroom do they find the meaning that makes their efforts worthwhile? The answer is they don't. Instead they fight the learning every step of the way by giving the least effort possible, avoiding the work, feigning ignorance, being absent, acting out, distracting others, and/or calling attention to themselves. And they usually drop out of school in large numbers.

What would be necessary for these young people to attach meaning to what they learn so that they become engaged, gain confidence in their efficacy as learners in the classroom context, develop demonstrable skills, and stay in school? We need to use teaching strategies that help them make meaning. That is not as easy as it sounds, however, because the educational ground has shifted under our feet in radical ways within one generation that necessitates a change in our view of learning and how it happens.

CHAPTER 3

Meaningful Learning in a Connected World

"We cannot solve our problems with the same thinking we used when we created them."

—Albert Einstein

The World *Has* Changed

I write these words at the end of the first decade of the 21st century. I have taught and worked in education now for 28 years. Just how much the world has changed in that time is highlighted by some of the points raised by educator Karl Fisch in his fascinating "Did You Know?" YouTube videos, which he first appeared in 2006:

- 25% of workers have been with their employer less than 1 year; 50% less than 2

- Today's learners will have 10 to 14 jobs by their 38th birthday

- Today's 21-year-olds have watched 20,000 hours of TV, played 10,000 hours of video games, talked 10,000 hours on the phone, and sent/received 250,000 e-mails or instant messages

- One out of eight couples married in the U.S. in 2005 met online

- The number of text messages sent and received today exceeds the population of the planet

- There are more than 540,000 words in the English language, about five times as many as during Shakespeare's time

- In 2005 the amount of technical information is doubling every two years; by 2010, it is predicted to double every 72 hours

- Predictions are that by the time children born in 2007 are 6 years old, a supercomputer's computation capabilities will exceed that of the human brain

The world of work has also irrevocably changed in the past generation. Harvard Business School professor John Quelch estimated in 2009 that the economic value of the Internet in the United States alone was at least $680 billion. This astronomical number for a technology that did not even exist when I started teaching! Below are a few jobs that did not exist back then:

- Blogger
- Online Community Manager
- Interior redesigners
- Green funeral directors

- Patient advocates
- Video journalists
- Social media strategists

Colleges and universities are also offering training for new career paths, such as:

- Organic agriculture
- E-business
- Nanotechnology
- New media
- Sustainable development

A survey administered by the business-networking site Ecademy suggests there are many others on the horizon like:

- Body part maker
- Nano-medic
- Pharmer of genetically engineered crops and livestock
- Old age wellness manager/consultant specialists
- Memory augmentation surgeon
- "New Science" ethicist

Many of the new careers require tremendous creativity, resourcefulness, and higher-order thinking skills. Authors such as Thomas Freidman have remarked that the nature of work for the majority of people in North America has irrevocably changed in the following ways:

- Global competition has taken many low-skilled manufacturing jobs to foreign shores

- There is less job security in any sector and most of the students in schools today will have multiple jobs/careers throughout their lives
- The "flat world" has made the ability to respond to change quickly and effectively, build alliances, and think creatively more important for employment success than ever before
- The environmental consequences of our decisions and actions are becoming apparent with each passing day and this will necessitate new thinking and innovation on a scale unheard of in the past
- To have the ability to contribute to society, learning will not be a "schooling" event, but a necessary part of every person's development—in both formal and informal settings

Given these changes, it's reasonable to think that the majority of new areas of employment may not even have been conceived yet.

To meet these employment challenges, certain skills are paramount. In Employability Skills 2000+, the Conference Board of Canada indicates that future workers will have to be able to do the following with ease and skill:

- Communicate
- Manage information
- Use numbers
- Think and solve problems

- Demonstrate positive attitude and behaviours
- Be responsible
- Be adaptable
- Learn continuously
- Work with others
- Participate in projects and tasks

Do your realize the challenges this presents to our current education system, a system originally designed to prepare workers for a nascent industrial society that required them to have basic knowledge, the ability to read and write, and show up to the factory on time? The very design of most school buildings and organizational structures reflects this: children moving from grade to grade, like widgets on an assembly line. At each level along the way the teacher is asked to present content and skills to be mastered. Quality control (testing and grading) assures they can "pass" on to the next grade. As we have seen, in the past, those who were unable to learn in this system left it, but there were broader opportunities for their success outside of it. Those who leave school before graduating today will not find such opportunities.

Because the purpose of this book is not to advocate wholesale change in present structure or complain about its deficiencies, but to help those who work in classrooms give all of their students what they need to succeed, and because we recognize that educators today cannot even pretend to know what kind employment they are preparing their students for, it is important to reflect on what tools will give their students the best chance at success in whatever context they find themselves. We have already identified that they need to complete high school and leave it with the belief that they can learn. The most significant step in accomplishing that has to do with understanding and appreciating one decisive fact— what has happened to education for content.

Content Education Is Dead

In the last century, much of school learning was based on what you knew. Memorization of facts, figures, dates, and formulas were all indicators of how well you were educated despite the fact that—even 100 years ago—these memorized items did not dramatically affect daily life. Today, the virtual world in which we live means that content is forever at our fingertips and flows through our lives like the air we breath. They have no meaning except in the context of how they are used. Schools are still grappling with this change, the challenge of which has only become apparent in the last 10 years. Yet most of the students in our schools have known of no other reality. If they want to discover something, information is literally at their fingertips. This sets up a disconnect that makes traditional classroom practices of purely teacher-directed lessons requiring students to learn and regurgitate content impossible to justify outside of busywork. Young people are savvy enough to know this, but the motivations highlighted in the Chapter 2 (internal attraction, desire to please, intrinsic motivation to achieve, or fear of consequences.) prompt most to go along with the process.

The result of our classroom learning in this context is like the proud homeowner who wants to show his guests his newest picnic table project, but when he brings them out back to see it, all they see is a pile of wood! He thinks he's finished, not realizing that the wood is only the starting point in creating a table. He then proceeds to regale his visitors with how he searched in the forest and took a lot of time to find exactly the right wood until one of them asks, "Bob, why didn't you just go to the lumber store?"

Bob's exasperated wife chimes in: "I tried to tell him that, but all he was interested in was finding the wood—and now we have no place to eat!"

Think for a moment about the content knowledge that has been so important to education—facts, figures, dates, etc. It is vital to learning, just as the wood is necessary for Bob's table. And we need to know how to get that "wood." We need to know where to look, what kinds there are, etc. But once we have the wood, we are not finished. We have to *do something* with the wood before it will become a table. To do that, we need to know how to manipulate the wood to serve our purposes. If all a carpenter can do is collect the wood and display it, and he spends most of his time doing that, he will not be successful no matter how nice his collection of wood. And it would be especially pointless if he could have gotten all of the wood he needed in a fraction of the time at the lumber store.

This analogy may seem silly and ridiculous to you, but much of our present education does exactly the same thing! Its prevalence is illustrated by popular TV shows like "Are You Smarter than a 5th Grader?" that imply the real learning done in the classroom is in the collection and stockpiling of knowledge. This may be great television entertainment, but for today's student, it is a poor focus for education. Students whose learning revolves around memorizing content, even if they are successful, will be as prepared for their futures as horse and buggy makers were for the advent of the automobile. They will not be equipped with the necessary strategies to be successful.

Long Live Content Education!

And yet, we should not discard the content because, like the wood in a table, it is necessary. It is the raw material that is useful in developing the skills that students need and the attitudes that will help them use these skills effectively. But it is not the only part of the learning process—and definitely not the most important. We know that just because someone has information at his fingertips, it's the ability to use that information that's crucial. Curricula throughout North America recognize this and encourage deep learning in areas like the following (which are actually the comprehension strategies on which students are tested in Ontario):

- Activating prior knowledge

- Visualization
- Finding important ideas and summarizing
- Evaluating
- Making predictions
- Making connections
- Questioning
- Drawing inferences
- Monitoring and repairing comprehension
- Synthesizing

These skills are necessary to develop the capabilities needed in 21st century workers and citizens. You will also notice that these skills are processes requiring a deep ability to manipulate information. They are also to a certain extent mysterious and subject to interpretation, and this has presented challenges to educators. They are much harder to "test" than whether someone knows who lost the battle of the Plains of Abraham or what the organs in the digestive system are. Most important, the demonstration of these skills requires a higher degree of student engagement and cognition than a simple memorization task. Yet we have seen that struggling students do not generally have either engagement or cognition in the classroom because there is no meaning attached to it for them. Ask a disengaged students to make an inference and see how far you get. So what can we do?

Meaningful Work

In his book *Outliers: The Story of Success*, Malcolm Gladwell identifies meaningful work as labor and effort that you are willing to throw your heart and soul into. He makes the case that immersion in meaningful work was the key to helping the most unlikely of people and families achieve amazing success. It has three characteristics:

- **Autonomy** – The structure of it allows one to control how to approach a task and make decisions about it without undue constraints

- **Complexity** – The task is challenging to the mind and requires ongoing adaptation and innovation

- **Close relationship between effort and reward** – It is clear to those engaged in it that if they put their effort into it they will see progress toward a goal that is deemed worthy in their eyes

Those engaged in meaningful work have a visible passion about what they are doing and often expend incredible amounts of time and effort on it.

Now think about the average classroom. How often are these three qualities present in the work children do daily? Rarely, in my own experience. And yet it eloquently explains to me why Rajhiv, a boy who did nothing in class for 5 hours in school, would spend 3 hours after school in the schoolyard, this time with a skateboard. But now he did expend effort: practicing the same difficult maneuver over and *over* and *over*.

He was trying to gain mastery with the skateboard through meaningful work. And what made it meaningful was that he decided on his goal and practice methods (autonomy), had set a goal for himself that required he learn new and difficult skills (complexity), and knew that to perfect the maneuver and impress his friends, it would require practice—lots of it. But he would know when he had attained it and his peers would give him instantaneous feedback ("Cool, man" or "Boy, that's lame!") and that was his close relationship between effort and reward.

Now hearing this, one is tempted to think, "Well that's fine for individuals on their own. He's able to do something he wants, but how could this realistically happen in a classroom of 30 children with different interests—not to mention widely different abilities, disabilities, and attitudes? Besides, skateboarding is a hobby and not in anything that will realistically serve him in the future. He may indeed be a great boarder, but he needs to do well in school too!"

This is my point exactly. Is it possible to take the characteristics of meaningful work so evident in Rajhiv's after-school experience and integrate them into the classroom so that Rajhiv will excel there as well? And if that happens, would he come to believe that he can learn in the classroom and even come to enjoy it and commit himself to learning? The answer is yes! And recent discoveries in brain science show us the way. It's what's happening in Rajhiv's brain that is causing him to see skateboarding as meaningful and class activities as meaningless. If we can change the way that he experiences classroom learning so that his brain attaches meaning to it, he will also behave differently in class. This is true of every child in that class. The key to this for a class full of children with different interests and abilities lies in the brain-friendliness of the strategies used. Let's take a look at how an approach can supercharge learning because it helps children learn in ways that make their brains keen for whatever material a teacher is presenting to them.

PART II

MAKING

KIDS

KEEN

TO LEARN

CHAPTER 4

Getting Our Heads Around the Brain Science

"Education today is a pre-scientific discipline line, reliant upon psychology (philosophy, sociology etc.) for its theoretical foundation. [The research presented here] explores the possibility that cognitive neuroscience might in due course offer a sounder basis for the understanding of learning and the practice of teaching."

—Organization for Economic Cooperation and Development, 2002

The Foundation for a New Approach

So far we have reviewed the challenges facing teachers and students in the classroom. We have examined the importance of staying in school and the fact that too many students do not finish their education, and many more are disengaged, not believing that the classroom is a place of learning, interest, or importance. We have discussed that part of the problem is the nature of learning in our connected era: Rote learning that stockpiles knowledge without fostering the skills to manipulate and interpret that knowledge is useless. Finally, we have identified that engagement, cognition, and cognitive intensity are essential to learning for students, but they cannot be fostered unless students attach meaning to what they are learning. The idea of meaningful work that combines autonomy, complexity, and a close relationship between effort and reward can pave the way toward strategies that help all students learn because it makes classroom learning extremely appealing to the brains of the students in the class.

It makes sense for all educators to become familiar with the important and revolutionary discoveries that brain science has made for their profession, because information about how the brain works can't help but make a teacher's job easier and student learning more effective. After all, the brain is the organ and instrument that makes it possible for each of us to learn, to teach, and to be taught. One of the challenges, however, is to describe the practical use of this research in a way that makes it useful for practicing teachers. Anyone who's faced a classroom of students knows the trouble you can get into when you try to apply theories disconnected from the gritty reality that exists when 30 students with different backgrounds, abilities, and interests come through your door. The responsibility that comes with the teacher's position—both for the safety and learning of the students—has been the foundation for the norms of the classroom that everyone is familiar with (desk work, teacher-focused, relatively quiet, etc.) And because these norms bring order that both teachers and students need, they often become the default starting point for every classroom. And yet, we know that this default approach alone does not providing meaningful learning for a significant number of students.

The practical benefits of brain-friendly strategies for both students and teachers are so great that they deserve serious consideration and application. The key is to examine how they can be embedded in the classroom without radical shifts that teachers would find unworkable. And that is what a KEEN learning approach does. But before describing the basis of this approach and the strategies that comprise it, we need to take a brief look at what exactly happens when the brain learns.

Brain Science 101 – A Cheat Sheet!

Powerful new techniques have been developed in the last few decades which allow scientists to be aware of the chemical and electrical reactions that occur in the brain when we think and learn. Technologies like Magnetic Resonant Imaging (MRI) have literally made it possible for us to see parts of the brain "light up" when they are used. What follows are some of the important understandings that have come from this research. Because of the practical nature of this book, these understandings are a summary, but the references can be found at the back of the book and are fascinating for those who have the time and inclination. However, here are a few of the important things that a busy teacher needs to know to understand KEEN learning:

The brain physically changes in response to experience. We think of our thoughts, ideas, or memories as "invisible," but they're not really. They are just hidden in our brain matter. When our brains think, tangible physical changes that take place as brain cells (neurons) signal each other by making new connections, or by strengthening existing ones. This is accomplished by electrical and chemical changes that allow neurons to talk to each other through connecting structures called synapses. This means that learning is achieved either through the growth of new synapses or the strengthening or weakening of existing ones. The brain's ability to be changed this way is called neuroplasticity. It also means that teachers *physically* change students' brains daily! Studies have revealed that neuroplasticity is extremely powerful, allowing the brain to rewire and even grow new neurons for functional purposes, even after injury or in old age.

Learning is about making neural connections in the brain. In her book *Brain Matters: Translating Research into Classroom Practice,* Patricia Wolfe writes that "all human behaviour can be traced to communication between neurons." These connections form networks that are able to communicate more quickly and effectively each time they work together. This forms the physiological basis for memories and it is why activities we do frequently do not require deep thinking—they just happen because neurons that "fire together, wire together" and become stronger and more efficient. We've all had the experience of driving home on our usual route and not even remembering the trip once we arrive; the path is so well worn both in our brains and in reality that we did it without thinking. Likewise, learning is most effective when teachers help students create strong neural pathways in the brain.

The creation of strong neural pathways involves both mind and body. It is natural for us to think that our brain functions as an independent computer that sits on top of our head and processes information. But when we reflect upon that idea, we know it does not hold true in our experience. You may have sat through Grade 9 geometry every day for a whole semester 15 years ago, but what do you remember from your many hours in the classroom? Very little...except for the day when you noticed an attractive fellow student looking at you and you tried to assume a suave pose but accidentally knocked everything off your desk—much to your chagrin and the amusement of your classmates. You remember *every* detail of *that* event even though it took place in an instant. Why? From a neuroscience perspective, you created an extremely strong neural pathway that was triggered by your emotions of embarrassment and frustration. Connections that neurons make are facilitated by a chemical cocktail of neurotransmitters, such as amino acids, dopamine, serotonin, endorphins, and cortisol, and they are triggered by emotions that help the mind decide what to focus on.

This structure of our brains and its effects on learning are extremely important for us. Neuroscientist Michael Gazzaniga estimates that 99% of the sensory data that comes into our brains is discarded. That is why you can sit at a city café near traffic and not really "hear" the car noise after a while. You can hear it, in reality, but your brain has decided it's not important enough to pay attention to on a conscious level. If we didn't have this filtering ability, we would never really free our minds to focus on anything, and we most likely would never have grown as the complex learners that we are. But the filtering system is very sensitive: If you were in the café and heard a loud screeching sound, you would immediately direct your attention toward it. This is because the brain's primitive warning mechanisms are kicking in to keep you safe, telling you to direct your attention toward something that might threaten your safety. In other words, the traffic sounds now *mean* something to you. As we shall see, emotions and bodily experience are extremely important for creating strong connections in the brain based on meaning and of particular relevance for students who struggle in the classroom.

Our brains are pre-wired for learning in certain ways at certain points. Despite the fact that the brain learns and changes until the moment of death, it appears to be better prepared to learn certain important skills at certain times. For example, children in every culture learn language at about the same time and the circuitry in the brain facilitates this. Over the course of evolution the brain has developed in such a way that it is "language ready" no matter what the language at that time. However, if language is not learned at that time, it becomes more difficult as time passes. So timing in learning can be important, as is the understanding that our evolution and genetic inheritance affect our ability to learn.

Remembering Where Our Brains Came From

The previous few pages are an admittedly cursory look at brain science and education; we will delve deeper when we talk about KEEN learning. But we have reviewed the most important things for teachers to understand: Brain science reveals that the brain is pre-wired to learn, that learning happens when the brain changes as a result of new neural connections, and that the strength of those connections is based on how important the brain determines the information (e.g., how much it means). Most importantly, the factors that influence the brain's determination have to do with emotional triggers.

And this is where it gets *really* interesting. The emotional triggers that affect us most profoundly come from the most primitive part of the brain, one that evolved over millennia with one purpose: to keep us safe and alive. They can trump everything and prevent the brain from focusing and learning in any context, but they can also drive incredible persistence and effort to learn. They are too powerful to be ignored, yet that is what happens in the classroom for many struggling learners and that is why our efforts to help them are often ineffective.

We live in a post-industrial and technologically advanced society but still carry the emotional wiring of our most primitive ancestors. Part of our success in advancing humanity has been solely reliant on our ability to deal with our primitive emotional instincts in a way that opens us to new and exciting possibilities. By exploring those possibilities—by dreaming what is possible—and having the passion and persistence to pursue those dreams, we move away from using the most primitive parts of our brains and call into service more complex ones. These frontal lobes of the brain, which developed latest in our evolution, differentiate us from other animals and make us human and are the ones that facilitate both personal growth and the advancement of society. They help us control our most powerful primitive emotion: fear.

Fear still stalks our struggling students each time they enter the classroom and prevents them from learning or even believing they *can* learn. What is this fear? Where does it come from? Most importantly, how can it be overcome?

CHAPTER 5

Fear and Loathing in the Classroom

"Fear makes strangers of people who would be friends."
—Shirley MacLaine

Classroom Learning Anxiety

As a young teacher, when I looked at the unengaged, underachieving students that were in my classroom, my first thought was not that they were afraid. Bored, listless, troublemaking, distracted, distracting, attention-seeking, lazy, and even dim might have come to mind—but not afraid! Now I see things much differently. I am convinced that a significant number of these students have what I would call *classroom learning anxiety.* This anxiety is not really about fear of learning any one thing, but a generalized unease with learning because the norms for success in the classroom feel foreign to these students. They experience the classroom as another planet in which their natural impulses and ways of learning do not seem useful. They may have the "disadvantaged" backgrounds that we referred to in Chapter 2 and have learned to trust what they learn from experience more than what they hear. They are most engaged when they are moving, experiencing, and "getting into" things.

As they progress through the school system, their natural learning styles are constricted because of the heavy auditory and seatwork orientation of the classroom. They find success in the classroom elusive socially because their natural social effusiveness conflicts with the requirement to sit still and stop talking for much of the time in class. They also come to understand that they have a fundamental character flaw: They are stupid and/or lazy. Not that anyone ever has to tell them that. They can see by what happens with other students and the teacher that they are not—both metaphorically and figuratively—making the grade. The anxiety begins with the sense that mastery in the classroom is beyond them. Without this sense they disengage emotionally and their brain searches for areas where they can achieve. There are good evolutionary reasons for this disengagement, and they are best understood in the context of a struggle between fun and fear, which represents two parts of our brains.

A Battle Between Our Primitive and Passionate Brains

Our ancient ancestors' very lives depended on them being successful at the things they attempted (hunting, gathering, farming), and the consequences for failure were dire. Fear of those consequences was an extremely useful tool; those who did not effectively respond to fear's promptings weren't around very long. It made people alert to when they were in danger, or when something wasn't working; likewise, when something *did* work, you did more of it and developed routines to make it easier. Once fear was allayed, however, humans were not satisfied. They dreamed, wondered, and looked for different ways to do things; contrary to the fear engendered with life-threatening situations, this dreaming was *fun* and the ideas it embodied became the basis for efforts to innovate and change things. Of course, this also provoked anxiety because the suggested changes might not work, but those people who were passionate enough to move beyond individual or collective fear often provided society and themselves with a new level of ability and understanding. It was, in essence, this tug of war between fear and fun that has characterized learning and societal progress throughout human history.

We have also seen that the intensity of that learning has a large part to do with emotional factors connected to meaning. It's now time to look a little more closely at what happens when emotional triggers influence learning. The amygdala, one of the most primitive parts of the brain, is the key player in this as it relates to the power of fear. Located at the base of the brain, it is small but powerful.

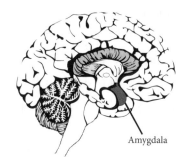

Amygdala

It is a gatekeeper that filters the input from our senses and evaluates whether or not it presents a threat to us. If so, it immediately triggers the release of chemical neurotransmitters that activate what is called the "stress response" readying us for fight or flight. A cocktail of chemicals are released into our bloodstream that cause the heart rate to rise, palms to become sweaty, and our visual focus to narrow. We experience this as being afraid. Much of this happens without any conscious thought, and with good evolutionary reasons. Imagine you were a villager walking through the forest picking berries and, all of a sudden, a tiger jumps out on the path. There is no time to think about it—it is necessary to act—*now*! So, before even being aware of it, you crouch, pick up a stone, hurl it at the tiger, and race away. You do not look back or even slow down until you emerge from the forest a few minutes later and collapse out of breath. But you are still alive—and your stress response has saved you—as well as the children, grandchildren, and other descendents that will arrive after you mate with that cute villager a few huts down.

Without the amygdala, you would have been lunch, so it's good you had it. Interestingly enough, all sensory information coming into the brain is simultaneously sent to the amygdala as well as the other areas of the brain that normally handle that input. I like to think of the process as similar to what happens when a child asks his parents to be allowed to do something as he heads out the door to play:

Child: "Hey, can I go parachuting off the roof at Billy's house?

Dad: "The roof? Mmm…How would you get on the—"

Mom: "NO!"

Both parents would reach the same conclusion, it's just that the dad finds the concept novel, worthy of seeking more information and the mother sees only the extreme danger. There's no time to debate—the decision is made immediately and irrevocably. That's what happens once the amygdala triggers the fight or flight response. The primitive brain is in the driver's seat, and only when the sensory input is evaluated as being safe will it relinquish control. The chemicals released also imprint the neural pathway associated with the event strongly enough that even the thought of it can bring a return of the fight or flight response.

This was what made fear such a useful learning tool for our ancestors; it told you where to focus your most intense attention. It was important to remember where on the path the tiger jumped out, because if that's where the tigers hung out and you did not pay attention to it, you probably wouldn't get a second chance. Thus, you would have a fearful feeling approaching that place in the future. Not only that, you might avoid that path—and possibly any path that was similar. If that proved impossible, your attention would definitely be focused on avoiding the danger and it would be a long time before you used the path again without being distracted by the feelings caused by your past experience. And even if the village elders told you that you should stop along the path because the best and most nourishing berries were there, it would not have much effect on you—even if you were hungry—because you knew firsthand that there were *more* important things to worry about than berries. And so, instead of berry-picking in the forest, you preferred to spend your time improving your hunting skills on the savannah because at least you could see what was coming out there, where you were the hunter and in control and could avoid the fear that came when unexpected things jumped out at you.

It is clear that while fear was important for survival in primitive times, it has only minimal value now, particularly in education. The use of the facilities of the frontal lobes will have much more to do with success in school than the amygdala because they are the source for the higher-order thinking that modern learning requires. And yet the neural stress response humans feel when threatened by something is still the same as if a tiger were chasing you. Even worse, Patricia Wolfe points out that humans can even be in prolonged chronic states of "fight or flight," which can have devastating effects on the ability to learn, not to mention bodily health.

It is my contention that the fight or flight response based on fear affects a large percentage of those students who don't succeed in the classroom. They rely more on the amygdala when confronted with educational challenges: fight (resistance or causing trouble in class) or flight (become listless, unengaged, and put forward minimal effort). And like the villager in the story, they turn their focus in learning in areas where they are more successful—and those are not found in the classroom.

But why are these students reacting this way to learning when others don't? Let's look at how their approach to learning changes as they age.

Early Learning

When you look at most toddlers and preschool children, the struggle between fun and fear is clearly present. Their sense of fun, exploration, and learning is apparent as they have tremendous successes learning to walk and talk, as well as to influence their environment and the people who populate it. Fear is necessary to avoid a few physical dangers, but nurturing parents help children to move beyond unnecessary fears, usually by talking with them and supporting them when they venture into potentially fearful areas. For the most part, though, learning is joyful and has many of the Gladwellian characteristics of meaningful work. Learning to walk is indeed autonomous and complex and represents a close relationship between effort and reward.

It is also clear, however, that how young children approach learning is also influenced by their unique personalities and interests (e.g., one child likes to play alone, another loves to seek out others, some like watching, and others jump into things as soon as they sense them). They learn most readily in the fashion that is most comfortable to them. An appreciation of these differences is the basis for the different learning styles/multiple intelligences that Howard Gardner and others have written about.

Gender Differences

There are also marked gender differences in learning styles. There is admittedly some debate about where these differences come from (i.e. nature or nurture). As well, the brain structure of males and females is said to be virtually identical. Nevertheless, how they use those brains—particularly in learning—is different and observable.

This was driven home to me clearly as I worked on this chapter on my computer in a local café. Here is a description of what I observed over 15 minutes: A mother and grandmother enter with five children for a snack—two girls and three boys, all around the ages of 5 through 8. "Now sit down and wait and I'll get you your treats," says the mother.

The girls sit down at one small table with the grandmother and the boys go to another nearby. The girls gaze intently as the grandmother shows them one of her rings and describes how it was given to her by their grandpa, who is "in heaven" now. The girls ask questions and listen as the older lady answers. She doesn't finish, however, as she has to look up and speak to the boys who are jostling each other at the other table. "Now you boys sit back down!"

The boys have not really sat down since they arrived at the table. They lean against the chairs, push each other, and laugh as they make funny faces saying things like "My butt hurts!" They get so loud that the grandmother says again, "You boys don't be rude or you won't get a treat!"

This appears to have little effect on the trio. The mother returns with a bag and says to the boys, "Here's your cookies, but you can't have them unless you sit down." They quickly sit down.

The mother turns to the girls who wait while she doles out the goodies. As she's handing the cookie to the last girl, the mother is surprised as one of the boys comes over and reaches into the bag from behind, trying to take his cookie saying, "Want mine!"

She pulls the bag away. "What did I say? Sit down!"

He sullenly sits. The boys are given their cookies; they sit quietly for a moment and chow down, while the mother joins the grandmother and girls at their table. They chat about what they are going to do afterward and the girls listen, asking questions.

The boys are no longer quiet—they are not even at the table anymore. They are wandering around the café, cookies in hand, touching the various displays. They start to struggle over a package of coffee, cookies in one hand and package in the other until one wins the battle and the other one cries "TOBY! You said mine!"

Both the mother and grandmother look over.

"Boys, I told you to sit down—now do it! If you don't behave we aren't going to the park after!" says the mother, slightly exasperated.

The boys slouch toward their table.

"But Toby took mine!"

"Did not!"

The scene continues for a few minutes until the entire group leaves. My guess is that they headed for the park, because then at least the adults would be able to talk and the kids would be occupied.

This experience—which is no doubt familiar to many parents—is quite indicative of the differences between girls' and boys' learning:

- The girls engage in conversation and social exchange to confirm their understanding, while the boys use their bodies to explore

- The girls' oral language skills are stronger than the boys, because they are used more

- The boys primarily use language to get immediate results such as laughter and recognition from others, something they want, or to appeal to authority for fairness; their bodies are used more extensively to explore their environment—often in a competitive way that seeks control or mastery

- The boys react to prompts of action better when they know what the results of those actions are likely to be; the more immediate, the better (i.e., sitting down quickly when it means they'll get a cookie)

If we accept the premise that people do what they do because they feel it works for them, it is easy to see that the boys' behaviour is reinforced by their experience and the rewards it brings them. In reference to the brain structure, the boys' neural pathways are strong in the areas of physical exploration and the girls in social exploration because they use that brain circuitry more frequently for their learning as young children. And although physically the brains of boys and girls may be the same, their wiring is different.

These observations are confirmed by researchers. Dr. Leonard Sax, who has compiled the results of brain research in his book *Why Gender Matters*, argues that the gender differences in the way the brain makes neural connections are profound in young children and have a tremendous impact upon learning styles. The most important differences include:

- Young boys have poorer hearing than girls (and thus often do not hear the teacher)
- Boys enter school up to 2 years behind girls in oral language development and fine motor skills because the parts of their brain devoted to these tasks develop more slowly
- The eyesight of boys is wired to respond to movement, location, direction, and speed, whereas girls' eyes discriminate and define objects in more detail
- The parts of boys' brains devoted to kinesthetic/spatial perceptions develop earlier and are much larger than those of girls

This is distinctly contrary to the belief that children are born as "blank slates" and it is only the way they are nurtured, which explains their preferences and behaviour. The nurturing is important—or all of us in education wouldn't have a job! But to be effective, *nurture* must be informed by *nature's* tendencies that are reflected in the way the brain is wired.

Why would these differences be so pronounced if, at birth, the brains are similar? We have to return to our evolutionary ancestors to understand that, in the same ways our brains have a built-in and genetically supported instinct for language, we also have them for other areas of learning. When we are young, many of these are gender-specific and due to the way that humans lived for many millennia. In primitive societies, males were responsible for hunting and defending the tribe. The skills required for this were:

- Ability to focus narrowly on important vs. unimportant sensory input

- Physical prowess and bodily skill were required for intense bouts of physical activity and effort, followed by long periods of little activity except for games that improved hunting skills

- Spatial-geographic sensitivity (it was important to know how far the animal was before you threw that spear)

- Aggression and risk-taking were important tools in hunting success, but were balanced against the rewards before being used

- Power is positional and won through demonstrating physical superiority and/or cleverness

In her book, *The Female Brain*, Lorraine Brizendine points out that females developed different skills:

- The ability to read faces and tones of voice, which protected them from stronger, potentially violent males

- A skill at verbal agility that compensated for less physical strength, allowing women to:
  - defuse conflict with men
  - mask aggression
  - build alliances with other women by speaking and community-building

- An innate sense of discrimination that allowed them to pay attention to the fine details of the environment that might present threats to their offspring

Female roles and child-bearing responsibilities necessitated the avoidance of risk and the ability to focus on low-intensity tasks over long periods of time; these attributes were necessary for survival.

At first glance, these differences might appear to have little relevance to our modern situation. After all, we don't live in primitive societies with the division of labour described. Our culture is much less violent and misogynistic. Women and men do most of the same jobs today. We raise our children differently than in days gone by. Gender differences have therefore been reduced considerably, but these changes have taken place relatively recently in evolutionary history. For most of the time humans have been on earth—and the time during which their brains developed—these gender differences were important and reinforced by the chemical makeup and wiring of our brains.

Do all children have these tendencies in equal proportion? No. There are of course variations, but observation reveals that for the majority of children, these tendencies do apply. In short, while the way that we raise and educate children helps rewire the brain differently in modern society, the brain's readiness to learn in its default gender mode is extremely strong. And it becomes more powerful whenever an individual senses danger or threat.

Why is this important? We have seen statistically that more males than females are dropping out of school. Education in schools has evolved to the point that it makes school more advantageous for girls and less so for boys. The strengths in oral language, the ability to navigate in social situations, to display prolonged attention to tasks over time, and the willingness to learn from teachers and instructors are increasingly necessary and valued in advanced industrial societies. And those skills are going to be the ones that are rewarded both socially and financially in the future. Boys' natural tendencies, while still useful in a farming and industrial society, become less valuable in societies where service industries are primary. Their risk-taking and ability to focus is indeed necessary but must be applied with increasing reference to the female soft skills. An awareness of this helps to clarify why all children do not move smoothly into the classroom.

Unsuccessful Students: A Journey from Fun to Fear

Let us look at what happens to young children as they experience school. By and large, the basis for their learning has been exploration, and this still continues in many kindergarten classrooms. However, as students progress through the school system, a transition in learning takes place: It becomes less exploratory, less experiential, more auditory, and, of course, biased toward reading and writing for success. The majority of students are able to make this transition because of their readiness when they enter school—i.e., a large neural network has been established in their brains to process oral language, and this forms the basis for a successful transition to reading comprehension and written expression. They are kept afloat through the challenges of this by the motivators of internal attraction, desire to please, intrinsic motivation to achieve, or fear of consequences.

But for others, particularly for certain boys who rely most on their natural tendencies, they meet less success in each grade. First of all, their lack of oral language skills causes them to fall behind. Then their bodily exploratory tendencies are curtailed; they must sit still for increasing amounts of time in situations where they cannot control their environment. If they rebel, they are punished with time-outs, withdrawal of privileges, visits to the office, and calls home to parents. They feel threatened and the amygdala often kicks in as they realize they cannot master what is expected. They increasingly focus their energies where learning is fun and successful for them, like recess and gym class. In my experience, by about Grade 3 many turn off for good. They may be there physically, but the fun in learning moves to areas outside of the classroom, like sports and video games, where they can feel success. The classroom has little meaning except as a place where one must avoid being put on the spot or cornered into doing things that seem impossible; classroom learning anxiety becomes a daily presence for these students.

Classroom Dynamics

In the classroom, we can find a situation where boys have a desire to play and win with mastery and control. They want to use a bodily-kinesthetic testing approach to learn because their experience dictates this is where they can get the quickest and most personally satisfying result. Efforts are disciplined to achieve that as directly as possible. Oral language is useful only insofar as it can help them achieve their goals; in this way it may be used manipulatively. They see rules as the way to make sure no one cheats.

Many girls, on the other hand, see power relationally, and seek to understand the social structure and its "rules" to see where they fit in. They use their oral language skills in social testing and work hard to develop efficacy in navigating that structure. If sitting quietly, doing one's work, and playing by the rules help them to do that, they are happy to do so. By and large, they are rewarded by verbal and visual cues that indicate they are doing the right thing and will be successful. In his book, *Boys Adrift*, Dr. Sax describes the educational situation that this creates:

> It's easy to see how these sex differences are relevant to education. Girls will do homework because the teacher asked them to. Boys are more likely to do homework only if it interests them. If it bores them, or if they think it's "stupid," they are more likely to ignore it...Even the highest-achieving boys are significantly less likely to do the homework than comparably achieving girls. Girls at every age get better grades in school than boys do, in every subject—not because girls are smarter, researchers have found, but because girls try harder...That divergence leads to an enduring paradox: at every age, girls do better in school but are less satisfied with their achievement, compared with boys. In 2006, researchers at the University of Pennsylvania reported that girls' greater self-discipline and self control—perhaps deriving from their greater motivation to please the teacher—appears to be a key distinguishing factor that enabled girls to survive and thrive in the accelerated world of twenty-first-century education.

We have a situation in which those who can work within the traditional classroom structure gain confidence through success in that structure, particularly where the norms of that structure are congruent with their natural tendencies. But those who do not, whose natural tendencies are different, have increasingly less success and put in less effort. This is surprisingly similar to what developing psychologist Martin Seligman terms *Learned Helplessness*, a condition he observed in rats when they lost control of their environment, which he believes can afflict people as well. Students with this orientation toward the school system leave it mentally, sometimes many years before they formally "drop out." Worse still, their sense of being able to learn in the classroom environment is very low and will affect their learning opportunities for the rest of their lives.

But it doesn't have to be that way. Through an understanding of how their brains are wired and the evolutionary tendencies that must be satisfied in struggling learners, we can find the key to bring these students back into the learning community with passion and achievement. They can again experience the power and joy that comes from learning in an environment demanding great effort in meaningful work that will excite them, develop their skills—and amaze their teachers and parents!

How can we get them so keen for learning? By acting on what we know.

CHAPTER 6

Leveraging What We Know

"Yeah... Miss Jones told me I was smart that I can do it, but I don't believe it. Teachers is paid to say that kind of shit. She don't know that I can't do it. When she tries to explain it to me, I don't get it. Then I know she's all feeing sorry for me and I hate it...I like her and all, so I don't cause no trouble here, but the sooner I get out the better."

—Grade 9 student

What We Know

We have seen that the traditional approach to learning has not been successful for a significant minority of children in the classroom. These types of students have always been with us, but there were more options outside of the classroom for them in previous eras, making classroom failure less of a life-limiting event. With the reduction of these external options for success, our post-industrial society relies more and more on education and classroom learning, and thus reduces the options that used to be available to these students. They need to learn and, more importantly, *believe* they can learn in the classroom or they are at high risk of dropping out of school, limiting their career choices, and living with a sense of inadequacy that can sap resilience and creativity for the rest of their lives.

It is also clear that for many who do succeed now, there is still an engagement and passion gap in their approach to classroom learning, and they often go through the motions in an education that provides them with simple facts, figures, and disconnected skills that will not serve them well in their improvisational future. That future will, at minimum, require our students to have the ability to manipulate information with skill and insight, to continue to learn throughout their lives, and to have the motivation and persistence to apply their learning in new and unpredictable ways. To trigger this motivation and persistence, students must engage in "meaningful work," which has been found to trigger passion and engagement in many who are high achievers. Yet, with its characteristics of autonomy, complexity, and a close relationship between effort and reward, meaningful work is precisely the element that is often missing from classroom learning.

Our exploration of recent brain research has revealed that learning only occurs when we construct neural pathways through synaptic connections and that the most effective learning exists where the neural pathways are strongest.

But, because of the electrochemical basis for these pathways, emotions and the powerful neurotransmitters triggered by emotions have a tremendous impact on the motivation to learn and the intensity of that learning. Our emotions are intimately influenced by the sensory input that our bodies experience as well as by our genetic makeup—something that has evolved over millennia and has pre-wired our brains to learn certain things easier and have natural learning tendencies. We have also seen the powerful role that fear can have in hijacking emotions, particularly acute when the most primitive part of the brain, the amygdala, triggers a stress response and the "fight or flight" syndrome. This reduces the use of the frontal lobes and makes the learning of higher-order thinking skills more difficult. Fear and lack of success in the classroom produce what I have identified as classroom learning anxiety in young students, evoking fight or flight impulses that make it even more difficult to engage in classroom material and learning activities. These students become increasingly disengaged as they mature in our schools.

Finally, there are indeed gender differences in learning approaches, and these differences are both physiological and pre-wired as a result of our educational past. The differences are why there has been a marked increase in the gender gap between male and female success in school. Girls' pre-wired tendencies toward verbal language, social accommodation, low-intensity persistence, and sensitivity to risk are exactly the things that make them likely to succeed in a structured school environment, be rewarded in that environment, stay in school, and obtain the educational credentials that improve their employment chances. At the same time, boys' tendencies toward physicality when learning, short-term focus, spatial awareness, lack of respect for authority, risk-taking, and later oral language development make it harder for them to succeed at the same level as females in the earlier years of school. Upon entry to school, boys' natural tendencies are tolerated at best but are most often actively discouraged in classroom settings. These gender differences do not hold true in every case but are frequent enough to account for the phenomena where males are significantly less likely than females to finish high school or go to college—particularly if they come from homes with poverty or family breakdown.

What Teachers Know

If you are a teacher, you know you have experiential learners in your class. They are kinesthetic, intrapersonal, challenging, or indifferent. Any year that you have a significant number, you know you leave class each evening more tired and less happy with your efforts and very concerned about the future of those students. And to make matters worse, there seem to be more of these students each year. You may also realize that you have very little leverage with them if they are not motivated by an internal attraction to the subject matter, a desire to please adults, an intrinsic motivation to achieve, or fear of consequences of classroom failure. You can "herd" them and discipline them, and they may like you and even try to comply with your requests, but you know deep down you are not teaching them, because they are not learning.

You are asked to differentiate instruction for them, but there are not many solid strategies to do this. Could the dearth of strategies be because it is so difficult to teach differently to 30 students whose individual intellectual abilities can range anywhere from kindergarten through high school? Or to kids who have language difficulties, a lack of parental support, psychological difficulties, learning disabilities, or the problems that children who grow up in poverty often exhibit (i.e., fatigue, hunger, absenteeism, etc.)? Not to mention the fact that your time with them in the classroom is extremely limited, once you factor in recess, bad-weather days, school trips, and assemblies—and time that you are withdrawn from the classroom for professional development to improve your teaching! The call for differentiation is nothing more than a pipe dream if it does not take into account the realities that the "blizzard of the classroom" presents to the teacher. So what would help you deal with these realities?

A Classroom with Leverage

In physics, "leverage" is created when a lever is used to move an object using less force than what would be required to lift it directly. Educational leverage is similar: It's something that can facilitate learning easier and more efficiently than direct teaching. Educational leverage can be something both simple and complex: making students "keen" to learn. Would the classroom not be a joyful and tremendously effective learning environment if the students couldn't wait to learn? If they were inspired to use all of their creativity to solve educational problems and if they approached learning like a game they couldn't wait to play?

It is a popular belief in our culture that leveraging passionate learning in the classroom only happens when students encounter rare, inspirational "hero" teachers. These teachers reach into students' souls and, with a combination of love, discipline, and grit, change young lives forever. Many of these types of teachers are lionized in television and film. This search for singular heroes does not present a helpful paradigm if we want to improve what happens in the classroom because it focuses attention in the wrong area.

There *are* differences in the effectiveness of teachers that are observable, but are they the result of character or something else? Let us consider for a moment where the real power of the "great" teacher lies. It is not just in their ability to build relationships of encouragement with students—most teachers do this. The real difference is that those students who are in that teacher's classroom *believe* what the teacher says about their ability to learn and demonstrate that belief through increased application to classroom tasks and demonstrable achievement. How do they develop that belief propelling them forward? More important, how do they keep it—even after they leave that teacher's classroom? The only way is if it is reinforced through continued success in classroom tasks, each one solidifying the student's sense of efficacy and building their resilience so that when they do have a problem in class they see it as a challenge they can meet and not a confirmation of their inability to learn.

So what students believe and experience in their own efforts to learn are more important than who the teacher is. What is important is what the teacher *does*: the educational experiences that he or she creates that facilitate the students' beliefs and success. This seems obvious, so why am I belaboring the point? Because great teachers intuitively sense what students need and create those learning experiences without often knowing why, or even what they're doing in a formal sense. Their power is based not in the personality of the teacher but in the technique that, consciously or not, created strategies that met the learning tendencies of a variety of learners, but in particular, the experiential learners. This is crucial if we are going to help struggling students.

The issue of great teaching is not a character issue—it's a skill issue. Almost all teachers enter the profession for the right reasons and have the requisite character. Professional development and acquisition of new strategies are part of the teacher's life. What if each teacher complemented their dedication and goodness with strategies that truly allowed them to differentiate instruction in the classroom, were simple enough to be learned by anyone and implemented in any classroom, required little beyond the normal curriculum materials, but proved effective with many types of students giving them both passion and cognition, while at the same time improving their oral language and higher-order thinking skills?

These strategies exist. I have seen them in action, and some of the most effective are included in this book. The reason they work is because they meet the learning styles of the students using them, giving their brains and emotions what they need to create meaningful work in the context of the daily curriculum. The educational leverage provided to teachers by these strategies is tremendous. They are even better for struggling students, helping them see learning as play, giving them a better understanding of content, concepts, and skills, and helping them believe they *can* learn in the classroom. This belief becomes reality in student achievement and becomes a self-fulfilling prophecy that builds up educational resilience and self-confidence in the learner, and that is the one thing that can bear them through the vicissitudes of school learning toward worthwhile goals they set for themselves.

They help create a *leveraged classroom* based on meaningful work, engagement, achievement, and the belief on the part of the students that they can learn. The difference between this type of classroom and a less effective one is summarized in the following chart:

Unleveraged Classroom	Leveraged Classroom
Learning is Teacher/ Textbook Focused	*Learning is student-focused but makes use of the teacher & textbook material*
Rote recording and recitation of content material	*Content material accessed when important*
Teacher observably busier than students	*Students observably busier than teacher*
Teacher presented content with little regard to student learning styles	*Facilitates learning in a variety of learning styles*
Little student choice in how students process learning	*Student choice in learning approach*
Large amount of time spent on irrelevant writing, listening to teacher, or other media	*Large amount of time for oral language development, interaction, and meaningful writing*
Students passive, enduring task at hand	*Students passionate about the task at hand*
Assessment is primarily pencil-paper	*Variety of assessment tools, including pencil and paper*
Students count the minutes until next recess break	*Students need to be reminded to leave for recess*

Why It's Vital to Know the Basis for Keen Learning

Hopefully you are now interested in hearing about these strategies that have so much potential. What are they like?

How do you use them? How are they different from techniques used in the classroom now? What subjects do they apply to?

However, it is very important to understand the foundation of the approach I am suggesting. When one first considers the strategies, it is easy to think: "Oh, they're so simple...what can they do?" or "This is just playing!" A flower appears simple and enjoyable from a distance, too, but once we peer beneath the surface and see what is happening, there is a great deal of hidden complexity involved. Likewise, your toes may look insignificant compared to your other body parts, but it would be physically impossible to walk without them! As for the dim view of play in learning, we shall see that *play with a purpose* has profound effects on learning.

An understanding of the principles involved in this learning approach is necessary for those concerned with classroom learning because they need to take seriously the idea that what we know about how the brain learns requires that we change our practice and take the next steps in the evolution of educational practice. Using the exercises without knowing why they work is using them ineffectively. The overarching skill that is the hallmark of good education is *metacognition*, the ability to think about our learning as we are doing it. KEEN learning is a profoundly metacognitive approach for both teachers and students. If teachers use it with great awareness of its potential, students will reveal and reflect on their tremendous potential while participating. If we do not approach it in this way, we may return to leeching instead of teaching.

Leeching and Teaching

Do you know what leeching is? It was a technique used by physicians from ancient times up until the 18th century to help sick people. Leeches are parasitic worm-like creatures that live by attaching themselves to a host and sucking out their lifeblood. To cure people, the doctors of the time believed that it was bad blood causing sickness and used leeches to suck out that bad blood. This technique occasioned a great deal of suffering and exposed the patient to even more disease, but doctors did it anyway. Why? Because they did not understand the role of germs in disease. The germs were always there, it's just that doctors hadn't learned to recognize them yet. However, once people like Antonie van Leeuwenhoek, Lazzaro Spallanzani, and Louis Pasteur made specific advances to identify them, the practices of doctors changed and became much more effective. That change was fostered by improved technologies like the microscope, which helped to prove that these invisible things really existed. These advances set the stage for improved medical practice by doctors and better health for their patients.

Brain research has revealed that much of what we believed about classroom learning has been well intentioned, but not accurate (e.g., people can learn just because teachers teach, rote memorization was a good route to understanding, emotion had little value in learning, there are no innate learning styles). These beliefs fostered educational practices that were not just ineffective but, for some 25% of students, hazardous to their passion for learning and their belief that they can—or should have any reason to—learn in a classroom setting. The strategies in this book are an effort to reduce that hazard and need to be seriously considered. Those who would dismiss this approach because it's new or different need to understand that it's based on our new understanding of how the brain learns. Just because the doctors of the 15th century didn't see the germs didn't mean they weren't there. In the same way, just because the understanding of how the brain actually works goes against what we may believe intuitively doesn't mean it's not true.

Educators—like doctors—have a professional obligation to use the best techniques available in the practice of their profession. Being well intentioned or likeable is not enough. Imagine you are a parent and your son has a fever. You are told that there is a great doctor at the new clinic who has an excellent reputation. When you arrive at her office, you discover she is friendly and welcoming but also wants to put leeches on your child's arm to "bleed" the fever out. When challenged about her methods, the doctor says that she knows all about that "germ stuff" but she doesn't put much stock in it because this method has always worked for her. Would you entrust your physically vulnerable child to her care?

How is it different entrusting emotionally and cognitively vulnerable children to the care of teachers who won't use methods based on brain research because they might be a bit out of their comfort zone or because they are different from traditional practice? It's not, and that is why you must understand the basis of KEEN Learning before considering the exercises.

CHAPTER 7

The Elements of KEEN Differentiated Learning

"%@#&!!, man…Now I'm ready to LEARN!"*

—A Grade 8 student from an inner-city class overheard explaining indelicately to a friend how KEEN strategies made him feel

What Does KEEN Mean?

The name of this approach is an acronym referring to the four elements in the following diagram:

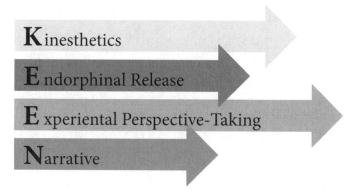

Kinesthetics

Endorphinal Release

Experiental Perspective-Taking

Narrative

Strategies that use these elements in combination create a learning experience that fosters stronger neural pathways in the participant by using different modalities and sensory inputs to link content and skills to cognitive understanding. In the process, it allows classroom material to be addressed to multiple intelligences and, in particular, the two intelligences that are least addressed in traditional classroom settings: kinesthetic and intrapersonal. Let's look at each of these elements to understand why they can be effective in triggering engagement and cognition

Kinesthetic Connections

Movement is vital to human beings from the earliest moments of life as a way to experience the world and communicate with others. Beyond that, it has been described as a default learning style for certain people. For them, bodily-kinesthetic movement serves as the primary gateway for learning and self-expression. Eric Jensen, in his book *Arts with the Brain in Mind*, argues that what he calls the "kinesthetic arts" are common and necessary forms of communication for all people that provide tremendous benefits:

> The Kinesthetic arts play a powerful role as a universal language, with a symbolic way of presenting the world. They let us communicate with others, demonstrate common human experiences, show insights, and solve common problems ... Kinesthetic arts enhance cognition, positive attitudes, and confidence; in some cases, kinesthetic arts *may grow new brain cells*.

He observes that if at one point in time a person learns both the name of the capital of Peru and how to ride a bike and then does not revisit that learning for 5 years, it is much more likely that the same person would have more success resuming bike riding than retrieving the capital name, and that the kinesthetic is the reason for this success.

What I find of particular significance about kinesthetics used in the classroom is the research that has drawn direct links between the parts of the brain that control movement and how that may influence memory and learning. The cerebellum, which has primarily been associated with motor skills, has recently been found to be important in long-term memory, attention, and cognitive functions that usually occur in the frontal lobe. One can imagine, knowing what we do about how the brain functions in males, that movement can be very powerful for them because it goes directly to their natural tendency to explore the world physically. Because it plays to his strengths, an activity that involves kinesthetics will not trigger classroom learning anxiety in a struggling learner. A boy who has been problematic in class because he is "busy" or will not sit down will enjoy the activity so much that discipline becomes simpler: The threat of removal from it is enough to encourage his self-discipline.

Even more powerfully, cognition and understanding of classroom material is aided by the "knowing" that a kinesthetic learner gets by using the body to represent that material. It becomes a physical allegory, symbol, or metaphor that brings the "a-ha" moment to the learner, giving an intuitive understanding with a flash of insight. From a brain-science perspective, this happens because the brain is able to use familiar well-used neural circuitry that supports and processes movement to access prior knowledge that students have experienced physically and link this experiential knowledge to the classroom material. They now have a cognitive peg on which to hang their learning. This creates *educational leverage* to help a struggling student understand in a moment what would have been impossible for them to comprehend in hours of auditory or visual instruction by the teacher. You can see it on kids' faces: "Ohhh...*that's* what she means!" Their eyes light up, they get very excited—and so does the teacher. A new neural connection has been made!

This is where the teacher's metacognitive use of the strategy is so important: Leverage is not of any use unless you use it. So when a teacher perceives the strategy is beginning to bring better comprehension and cognition, he can ask the student to explain that understanding. Doing this will help improve the child's oral language abilities, call into play their frontal lobe, and strengthen the brain circuitry around the concept being studied. By probing and testing the child's understanding, the teacher can modify any misconceptions and also offer genuine praise and encouragement, not an ersatz version that isn't really based on the child's achievement. The honesty of the feedback will be perceived by the student and begin to build the feeling that "*I do know this stuff!*" That in turn will create an emotional connection triggered by feelings of pride and efficacy, which will further strengthen the synaptic connections and neural pathways related to that learning. Asking the student to write something about what they know is now much more reasonable and easier for them because they get it and may even begin to sense *"....this stuff is kind of fun."* And that sense is important enough in itself.

Endorphinal Release and the Power of Play

It has been said that play is an essential part of life, not just for humans but also for many animal species. Stuart Brown, a researcher who has studied play for three decades, describes how the need for play can even be more powerful than the most basic of biological needs. He relates a story of how a team of sled dogs in the far north encountered a gaunt and hungry bear one afternoon. The bear moved toward the dogs, appearing ready to attack. One of the dogs, on seeing the bear approach, adopted a playful stance with his back arched, paws out in front and ears back. The bear stopped and then proceeded to play with the dog for the next half hour, rolling around in the snow with wild abandon. The bear returned every evening for the next week to do the same, before finally disappearing— presumably to continue his search for food! Likewise, Brown asserts that play is a powerful need for humans because it provides states of happiness, generates social relationships, spurs creativity, and is a "catalyst" for problem-solving.

Why is play so powerful? Researchers Kerr and Apter describe play as a *"paratelic* state of mind," rather than a behaviour. In this state of mind, there is a "protective frame" that allows for the individual to have greater control over his or her environment and take non-threatening risks in exchange for the excitement and stimulation that comes from the play. They argue that play serves both individual and social functions, namely:

- Learning and self-actualization
- Creativity
- Coping with stress
- Coping with change
- Maintaining internal stability within a group

For students in the classroom, this view of play is powerful, because within its "protective framework," they can exercise a level of control over their classroom experience through the use of their imaginations. Struggling learners often believe they have little control over their learning in the classroom. It's "done" to them and they passively endure or actively push back or try to find distractions. The autonomy provided by a playful activity can become the basis for generating meaningful work for that student.

More importantly, the enjoyment of play can cause chemical emotional reactions in the brain that affect the learner. The laughter generated by the playful aspect of KEEN activities is one of the most common results. Laughter has been associated with reducing stress levels and general overall health improvement. This confirms the intuitive feeling we have when a good laugh makes us feel better and helps put our problems in perspective. This could be caused by the release of endorphins that occurs when we laugh.

The act of play itself seems to provide differentiated experiential benefits to those who participate. Stuart Brown describes fascinating examples in the animal kingdom where play provides one thing for bears (improvisational skills in an ever-changing environment) and another for cats (the skills necessary to socialize). With a variety of differing groups of people, psychotherapists Blatner and Blatner have used dramatic play to satisfy both the needs of the group and the needs of the individual at the same time, observing that "whereas in many task-oriented groups, the personal idiosyncrasies of the group members are ignored or suppressed so there can be a unified effort, in play groups those elements of difference are welcome additions to the process." This is one of the reasons that KEEN activities work so effectively for differentiation in the classroom—in their playful aspects they allow for students of different ability levels to learn effectively together.

And the benefits are cognitive. Play enriches cognition and builds stronger neural pathways because it easily allows learning through non-threatening trial and error. Even more fascinating is the idea that there may be a vital cognitive advantage to using play that is somewhat counterintuitive: *Play makes the brain work harder.* First of all, the endorphins released during play and laughter stimulate your brain's frontal lobes; this leads to increased focus and attention span. It is then that play can do its work, according to Stuart Brown:

> Play is nature's greatest tool for creating new neural networks and for reconciling cognitive difficulties. The abilities to make new patterns, find the unusual among the common, and spark curiosity and alert observation are all fostered by being in the state of play. When we play, dilemmas and challenges will naturally filter through the unconscious mind and work themselves out.

He further argues that play spurs us on to mastery, which requires us to learn and experience new things.

We can see this in the lives of those great achievers who work incredibly hard but love what they do. For many people who engage in Malcolm Gladwell's concept of meaningful work, they are actually engaging in play! It is psychically rewarding despite the work involved. Remember, effort and difficulty are not what makes work unappealing to young people who struggle in school. The "lazy" students will often work very hard on the soccer pitch, in a video game, or in preparation for an automobile license exam. These forms of work are meaningful for them. And so it is through the use of play that KEEN strategies are designed to give classroom material meaning even when it does not come intrinsically from the student.

Before moving away from this element, I think it is useful to highlight a benefit of play for teachers and classroom environments. We have seen that both success and laughter build rapport, empathy, and affinity among human beings. The teacher who allows play in the classroom will not only laugh more herself, but will no doubt be surprised by the creativity, love of learning, and depth of knowledge her students will exhibit. Her preconceived notions of what they can do are surpassed by what they actually accomplish. She will be able to stand shoulder to shoulder with her students exploring and achieving rather than being face to face with students who push back whatever she tries to advance. Her job will become *fun* because she is accomplishing the vocation that called her into teaching in the fist place: having young people learn and grow because of her presence and efforts. It is now time to turn to what is perhaps the most powerful ingredient yet: The opportunity that KEEN activities provide for imagination and perspective-taking.

Experiential Perspective-Taking

The exercises in this book call upon students to use their imagination and allow participants to pretend to be other than what they are in "reality." The power and value of fostering imagination is given short shrift by many because its unreality is seen in contrast with the real business of everyday life—particularly in our era of standardized testing and accountability. But Albert Einstein, one of the greatest scientific minds of all time, reminded us of its importance: "Imagination is more important than knowledge. For knowledge is limited to all we now know and understand, while imagination embraces the entire world, and all there ever will be to know and understand." He lived well before our current interconnected world, but he recognizes the broad purpose of education that needs to prepare students to face the worldwide challenges of our era. We see that we are surrounded by the results of the unreal world of our imaginations—everything humans create comes from an idea. Steven Covey puts it well when he observes that "everything is created twice, first in the mind, then in the space we call reality."

Imagination is an important pathway to emotion. Mary Helen Immordino-Yang, former school teacher turned cognitive neuroscientist, asserts that modern neurobiology has confirmed the idea that humans are essentially emotional and social: "The very neurobiological systems that support our social interactions and relationships are recruited for the often covert and private decision-making that underlies much of our thought. The power of emotion has a direct impact on learning and cognitive function." She goes on to point out that studies with the mentally impaired have suggested that emotion may help to "tag" and reinforce memory and may be essential to the ability to make inferences and apply what is learned in one context to another. Other neuroimaging research has reinforced this link between cognitive function and emotion.

This research suggests two things: First of all, an enjoyable class activity can bring emotional benefits and a better attitude toward events that happen after the class has ended. As well, however, it suggests the possibility that an enjoyable activity using dramatic imagination may help to reinforce the ability to remember and learn.

The power of imagination and emotional memory is so powerful that it has been found to function even when other memory systems have failed. In "Remembrance of Emotions Past," Joseph Ledoux, a professor of neural science at New York University, posits this as true because there are really two brain-based memory systems: an implicit amygdala-dependent emotional (which, as you remember, is the oldest and most primitive part of our brain) and the hippocampus-dependent, which deals with an explicit memory of an event. The relation of this to KEEN activities lies in Ledoux's claim that when we recall something with an emotional link, the implicit and explicit memories fuse and "new explicit memories that are formed about the past can be given new coloration as well." Suppose a student struggles with a concept or skill in the past and is unengaged, in full "flight" from it due to lack of success. Using imagination playfully to approach it can create a more positive emotional reframing, which can overcome the perception of past experience.

There is another way that imagination can impact memory retention. Although there has been much debate about how it works, there is a general consensus that bizarre events stay in our memory. If that is true, then the regular appearance of the bizarre in a KEEN activity helps memory. The dissonance and contrast illustrated by the bizarre is often a source of laughter and mirth, which also seem to help jog memory function.

KEEN activities help students create imaginative metaphors around curriculum material, which engages the power of what Elliot Eisner calls "representation" where "evanescent" or fleeting thoughts are made concrete through self-expression. Arnold Modell contends that it is only our imagination that allows us to function in the world because it helps us pull together a plausible reality from the ever-changing blur of events and stimuli that we experience daily. Through the use of metaphor, the brain creates meaning, and we know how vital that is for helping the brain create neural connections that will retain learning. Modell also notes that emotion has been found to stimulate a wide area of the brain across both hemispheres, and because our imaginations can spur profound emotions, it is quite possible these emotions spur this increased activity.

At the experiential level, research has indicated how important context is to learning, even to the extent that students have been found to score better on tests in the same room where they originally learned the material. KEEN strategies help create improved context by allowing students to take different perspectives and thus provide the ability to interact with curricula using both imagination and experience, which improves alertness by making connections between the past, present, and future. When a child imaginatively "becomes" the hypotenuse of a right triangle, he is given a unique perspective that uses his imagination to experience what it means to be such a thing. His brain now has another set of connections that support the neural circuitry related to triangles. He becomes *part* of his learning in a way that creates significance and meaning. He now has a new, more personal "story" about the triangle. Let us explore why having a story is so important.

Narrative: Accessing Our Most Powerful Tool For Learning

Stories are an integral part of who we are. As young children, we love stories; as we age, we reflect on our stories. We not only reflect, we write them in our psyches. Much of our attitude toward our lives can be attributed as much to our interpretation of events as to the events that actually occur. We all have a story in our head about who we are and how our lives should proceed and we are most unhappy when the events in our lives do not support that story! Because narrative is such a primitive form of learning, understanding, and appreciating our existence, it can be a powerful part of learning in the classroom.

Famed psychologist Jerome Bruner asserts that narrative is the basis of our memory and learning. What we remember is in a narrative mode because that allows us to make sense of all the information we experience: "Self is a perpetually rewritten story. What we remember from the past is what is necessary to keep the story satisfactorily well-formed". It has been further argued that the more fully developed our narrative is, the more fully developed we are, and that the use of a personal narrative helps to bring unity to our understanding of life. It forms the basis for our earliest learning as preschool children. Stuart Brown emphasizes that this occurs because play is fused with narrative: "Play's process of capturing a pretend narrative and combining it with the reality of one's experience in a playful setting is, at least in childhood, how we develop our personal understanding of how the world works."

David Booth has seen this power at work with children in the classroom when they are allowed to create stories using drama. They inevitably become a closer, more cohesive group, develop better social skills, and bring more passion to their learning. In dramatic "story drama" there is a tremendous potential for satisfying personal growth when "the context is fictional, but the emotions are real."

KEEN activities benefit from this approach, helping students create an imaginative narrative that allows room for autonomy and complexity. They also create a close relationship between psychic efforts and psychic reward because they provide students with a way of constructing self-created meaning around curriculum material. This is very important in understanding the power of these activities for differentiating instruction. We have already reflected on the challenge a teacher faces when trying to help a classroom full of different students learn effectively. This is often because the presumed source of learning is solely the teacher when, in reality, learning only occurs when neural pathways are created in the students' brains; the teacher can only facilitate this.

Since we know that learning is most effective when it has meaning for the learner and that all learners are different, it is easy to see that it is nearly impossible for the teacher to create meaning for every child from the front of the classroom. It can be done, however, when each child can—in concert with classmates—create a story about the material *that makes sense to them*. Because narrative is such a powerful form of learning, this story has far more resonance with students and is more likely to be retained than anything the teacher could create.

Because KEEN activities orient learning toward the students' brains, they avoid the singular problem with teacher-focused learning: the fact that teachers' brains work harder in the process than *students'* brains. Many teachers work exceedingly hard to come up with ways to make curricula interesting, in essence, trying to weave a story that will "hook" their students. That work causes increased synaptic connections in the teachers' brains and strengthened neural pathways for them, but does not call forth the same level of cognitive effort from students, because all they are doing is accepting the teacher's story! As well, we know that not all of the students will buy into the teacher's story. On the other hand, KEEN strategies both reduce teacher workload and increase cognitive intensity among students by enticing them into the complex work of creating their own narrative and thus making a self-connection to their own "zone of proximal development."

Putting Them Together

It's clear that each one of the four elements described above has great potential for engagement and cognition among students. When you combine them the effect is compounded, increasing the opportunities for synaptic connections and the students to experience the task at hand as meaningful work. Sometimes the classroom activities described in the next chapter do not use all elements together, but they always involve at least two. As well, there are variations and extensions of the strategies, which allow additional elements to be added after the activity is familiar to the students. Once teachers are familiar with KEEN strategies, they will no doubt begin to come up with ideas on how to create their own variations or new exercises. As you will see, the strategies are not difficult or ground-breaking, they are just what I have discovered to be effective vehicles for embedding *Kinesthetics, Endorphinal Release, Experiential Perspective-taking* and the *power of Narrative* in the classroom setting. Any classroom activities that include these characteristics will offer the same benefits, provided that the teacher uses them purposefully and metacognitively.

Why They Work

KEEN strategies are successful because they provide the criteria for meaningful work connected to the curriculum (autonomy, complexity, and close relationship between effort and reward); they leverage learning by addressing a variety of learning styles within the context of one activity; and they keep students—and their brains—considerably more engaged, helping improve their oral language skills in relation to curriculum and allowing for multiple avenues of assessment for that curriculum. Most importantly, they move learning away from a sole focus on the teacher to a focus on groups of students who work together to reduce the *cognitive diversity* in the class. What this means is that, in any group of students, the individuals will be at different places on the knowledge and understanding continuum vis-à-vis what is being studied in the curriculum. Some will know almost all of it, while some will know next to nothing. The beauty of KEEN is that it creates conditions for students to work together to enhance their learning and develop efficacy and community in the class. The following diagram illustrates what happens in a traditional class when the teacher is only the "sage on the stage":

We know that the "bouncing" arrows include not only the disengaged and uninterested students but also those who, because their learning style may be more kinesthetic and intrapersonal, cannot comprehend best in an auditory or visual fashion. KEEN learning fosters more engagement and

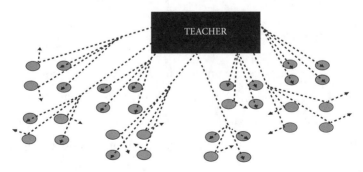

cognition and increases transfer of knowledge from the more knowledgeable students to those less so with the teacher as arbiter of accuracy and source of clarification.

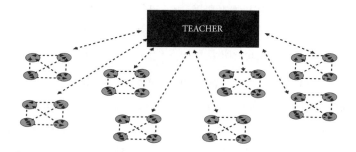

Thus the cognitive diversity is reduced. It's important to understand that within KEEN activities, we are not talking about peer tutoring as much as teamwork to reach the desired level of cognition and competency.

The Dramatic Connection

Those readers who are familiar with improvisational or "process" drama will undoubtedly find similarities in many—though not all—of the KEEN strategies and wonder why they are not presented as such. I also have a great deal of respect for the power of drama for learning and, indeed, already wrote a book on it (*Literacy Through Drama*). Advocates of drama in education are passionate and effective; however, for the vast majority of teachers, students and the general population, the word "drama" conjures up images of performance, frivolity, esoteric talent, and an ethereal pastime that, beyond its value for public speaking, has very little connection to the daily realities of most people; certainly, compared with the real subjects of language, math and science, it is considered a frill at best. Based on my experience, it is very hard to change this perception since drama has only infrequently been applied to these subjects by a few pioneers. Because of that, most educators do not view drama as a viable learning tool for the classroom.

However, my classroom work and research have convinced me that because of the power these activities can bring to classroom learning, they are too valuable to be left on the sideline. Thus, KEEN Differentiated Learning distills the essence of these activities, removes any performance or presentation requirement, values them for their ability to create synaptic connections fostering engagement and cognition, and specifically focuses them on the serious business of classroom learning. No artistic ability or inclination is needed to use them effectively.

A vitamin analogy might be useful. We know that we need to consume certain vitamins to stay healthy. Vitamin C is an important one, and oranges are good source of it. But what if we don't like oranges? Are we doomed to scurvy? Of course not, because we can get it from other foods like grapes, bananas, cauliflower, rosehips, or even taking a vitamin C supplement. A classroom that is healthy for students—especially struggling ones—will contain the elements of KEEN learning, as they provide essential nutrients for student learning and growth. Now let's go to the next chapter and see how easy it is to take these vitamins!

PART III

SIX

SIMPLE

STRATEGIES

TO KNOW

CHAPTER 8
The KEEN Strategies

"Education is what remains after we have forgotten everything we have learned."

—Marquis De Halifax

The Six Strategies for KEEN Learning

We arrive now at the description of KEEN strategies that can be used immediately in the classroom. They do not need any new materials and can be used with almost any curriculum context. Some are more effective with certain types of learning than others or work best at certain age levels, which I will highlight accordingly, but they have all been classroom-tested with thousands of students and teachers. The strategies are:

1. Still Life
2. Back and Forth
3. Brain-Writer
4. Handy Memory

5. Three-way Conversation

6. Connect Scenes

Most of them have variations and extensions that will be described.

Why only six strategies? There are no doubt thousands of effective teaching techniques available for classroom teachers and after all of the focus on brain science and educational research, I'm only offering six? How can they be useful in the variety of contexts found at the primary, junior, middle, and high school level? Well, let me ask you to consider today's modern classroom: How many different types of technological hardware are available to the teacher? Computer, overhead projector, CD/cassette player, TV/VCR/DVD player, LCD projector, a "smart" board, maybe…Can you find many more than six? I can't. Why aren't there more? With those tools you can access pretty much everything that you would need for class communication in terms of media. They are not to be the focus of the classroom, they are just tools to *support* the learning. In the same way, these KEEN strategies provide everything you need to transform your classroom—especially for struggling learners. Are there others? Yes, but they only make sense once you are using these basic ones.

The great irony of the information age is that more information causes people to pay attention less. The same is true for educators. Six strategies do not seem too hard to handle if they are easy to use. Finally, if there are just six, teachers may try a few; even two or three will make a huge difference to the students in their classrooms.

How To Use These Strategies

KEEN strategies are not meant to take over classroom practice in the same way that the overhead projector does not (hopefully!) define a teacher's classroom practice. Like the use of spice in cooking brings forth the true flavours of the ingredients, KEEN is meant to be used alongside traditional teaching methods to strengthen student understanding of curricula and make the experience more palatable, particularly for students who have hitherto refused to sample the educational buffet offered to them. They are designed to take anywhere from 2 to 15 minutes in a 40 to 60 minute class once the teacher and student are familiar with them, although they can be used longer if so desired.

They are particularly helpful where special education or ESL students are integrated into the classroom. They can also be used in a targeted fashion during a general classroom work period for small groups of students. The strategies are useful to evaluate students' prior knowledge, introduce new material to them, have them gain a deeper understanding of concepts or skills, improve memory retention of taught material, review for standard-type tests, or to be used as formative or summative assessment tools. I would strongly suggest you refrain from rewarding "performance" by praising it or asking students to applaud other groups. Remember, KEEN strategies are utilitarian classroom tools (how often do you ask for a round of applause for the overhead projector?). Despite the lack of emphasis on "performance," they are presentation tools and—

after the curriculum goals have been met—they can also be used, if desired, by willing participants who might like to share their knowledge with other students, staff, administrators, or parents. In the end, how a teacher uses them is his or her decision. What is important is that they are used.

Preparing Students for KEEN Activities

When using the strategies included in this program, it is essential that the teacher is confident that his or her students will remain in control, safe, and be responsive to instructions and directions, allowing the teacher to meet curriculum goals. *Freeze, Slo-Mo, and KEEN Classroom position* are techniques that help achieve this. Here are some techniques to ensure that students are ready to learn using KEEN strategies:

Freeze

Have students understand what is meant by "freeze." Students must stop exactly where they are and hold positions without moving or making noise for at least 5 seconds. The teacher can count down aloud from 5; for younger students, use your hand to show how much time is left before they can relax and move.

Use a signal. I usually just say "freeze" at medium volume and wait a few seconds. Students who hear it or see other students frozen immediately freeze themselves. A good way to encourage this is to tell the students during a normal classroom work period or even during an indoor recess you will say "freeze" softly and there will be a reward if the whole class can be frozen within 3 seconds. Teachers who use a bell or other technique to get their students' attention during class can also make that the cue to freeze.

It is important that the students actually stop moving and stop making noise when the teacher signals them. For some students, this may be very difficult after an engaging activity and must be practiced. Ensure that all students freeze by giving positive feedback to those who are completely still, while ignoring those who are not frozen. Do not move onto the next activity if the students cannot demonstrate an ability to freeze when it is called for.

Slo-Mo

Whenever the students need to move from one place in the classroom to another, or before and after a KEEN activity, have students move in slow motion. For kinesthetic children, this is beneficial because although it allows them to move, it forces them to concentrate on how they move. Most kinesthetic learners will actually put a great deal of effort into this!

Slo-Mo can be used to transition students into or out of a KEEN activity and is useful within the activities for control. Teachers who don't already use slow motion movement with their students often find this technique so useful they use it outside of KEEN to help students line up, enter the classroom quietly, or organize into groups.

Classroom Readiness

Many of the KEEN activities require a small area for a group to work. In a classroom where students are already placed in groups, this area is usually created without having to move furniture farther, as is illustrated in the diagram below.

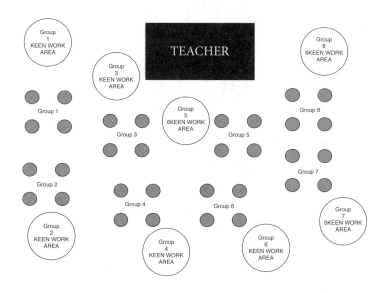

If the classroom layout does need to be changed to give groups small areas to work in, it is best that this be facilitated by having the students move the desks into the desired positions in complete silence after you say something like: "Please move into your KEEN groupings." In the next 30 seconds, the students move the desks and themselves —silently and without talking—into the pre-arranged positions and sit down and look at you, awaiting further instructions. If this is challenging for the students, practice it before introducing any KEEN activities requiring small-group work.

CHAPTER 9

STRATEGY I
STILL LIFE

This group of jocks swaggered into Grade 10 English class and assumed their regular position at the back of the class, slouched down in their chairs, looking bored. Only their English teacher's review of Death of a Salesman *stood before them and the football practice that would start in an hour and they showed no inclination to put any effort toward anything before then. When the teacher tried to get them involved in the discussion, they answered in monosyllables and rolled their eyes. After 10 minutes of KEEN activity these same students were folding their bodies into incredible positions, using them to represent the relationship between Biff and Happy. When asked into explain what they were representing, the teacher had to admit that their understanding was much deeper than any other students' in the class had demonstrated in the previous 15 minutes of discussion.*

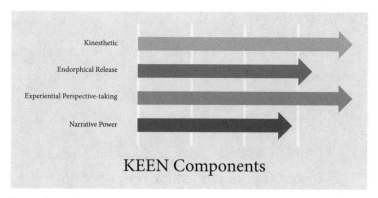

KEEN Components

Introduction

E asy to use as basic technique for helping students use their whole bodies for understanding, it also works well to help students understand and represent even very complicated concepts and processes. Still life is an effective tool that teachers can use throughout all areas of the curriculum to activate prior knowledge, teach content, deeply understand characters from literature and historical figures, and review information already taught. It is a good starting point for introducing KEEN strategies because it allows no movement or noise from the students.

Why STILL LIFE helps struggling students

- Permits movement while still connected to the curriculum
- Allows boys to process oral language while using bodies
- Allows for deeper understanding by linking kinesthetic representation with frontal lobe processing required for higher-order thinking

The Strategy Basics

A still life is a frozen picture that depicts a scene or an idea that the students create using their bodies. A good still life has the following elements:

- No movement or noise at all
- Different levels or body positions to represent the concept (e.g. standing, sitting, lying down, etc.)
- Good facial expressions and use of the body to express character or purpose
- Those who represent inanimate objects such as trees or rocks should close their eyes

Individual Still Life – Done alone by students, standing scattered apart or beside their desks, facing the teacher.

1. Ask the students to demonstrate with their bodies their understanding of the following:
   - different emotions
   - persons/places/things
   - concepts/ideas
2. Only allow the students 5 seconds to think about what they will display. Countdown from 5 and then say freeze.
3. After each still life, have the students return to a neutral position—no expressions on their faces, standing still with their hands at their sides.

Group Still Life – Done in groups of 2-6 (4-5 is optimal).

When creating still life with two or more students, it is important the participants cooperate so that the image created is both accurate and interesting. Use the same criteria for the Individual Still Life, but make sure to emphasize that as many people as possible be at a different level. Ask the students to make still life of:

- different emotions
- persons/places/things
- concepts/ideas/events
- steps of a procedure
- parts of a whole

After each still life, have the students return to a neutral position: sitting or standing in a circle, with no facial expression.

Tapping In – Use this technique to leverage better understanding and metacognition when using both kinds of *Still Life*.

Individuals can be asked questions of varying difficulty to determine what the student understands about what is being represented. If the students are portraying people or characters, they can be asked what they are feeling, or what they are thinking. If the students are portraying objects or concepts, they can be asked how their still life demonstrates that object or concept accurately. This is very effective for developing deeper understanding for both the students who are tapped as well as for those who are observing and listening.

1. When students are frozen, tap one on the shoulder and ask questions. The "tap" means the student can speak. Other students in the still life can turn their heads to listen, but should remain in position. Questions like these can be asked:

    - Who are you?

    - What are you doing?

    - What are you feeling?

    - Why are you feeling this way?

    - How could your situation be changed or improved?

    - Why are you an important part of your story?

2. Keep questions short—remember that it takes a lot of concentration for the others to remain still!

3. Once the questioning is finished, the student freezes back to his or her original position

KEEN Considerations

- Before introducing *Still Life* with curriculum, practice with things the students are interested in (e.g., sports, music, video references) critiquing the students on how well they stay still, use different levels, cooperate, and, of course, represent what they have been asked to illustrate.

- Students may talk in the 5 seconds used to create the still life, but keep it short at the beginning so that they are forced to make quick decisions together. This will encourage ego-restraint, build teamwork, and help them trust their bodily instincts.

- Oral language can be strengthened by allowing longer time for a group to provide a series of still life pictures that, for example, describe a process. This will require students to talk about how best to describe that process

- For more in depth *Tapping In*, or to use it as an assessment, without making the rest of the class freeze at the same time, a group of students can be invited up to the teacher's desk separately to display their still life.

- *Slo-Mo* can be added to any still life for better representation purposes.

Variations That Deepen Learning

- Participants in the still life are asked to rotate so that the still life *looks* the same, but they are in different places and taking different perspectives. If "tapped in," they must speak from those perspectives.

- After everyone has practiced each spot, tap in with each person speaking from the perspective of the part of the still life they are representing. Ask different questions of varying difficulty to assess the students' knowledge.

- If the students are demonstrating scenes or a series of still life, have one person step forward to narrate what is happening in the still life. Each still life should have a different narrator so that one student in the group is not the only person talking.

General Cross-Curricular Applications

- Represent vocabulary being studied in language, science, history, geography, or math
- Scenes from literature, e.g., novel, short story, picture book, poetry (summarizing using beginning, middle, end, OR First, Then, Next, Last format, OR any other formats used for retell/summary)
- Steps or procedures in science or in procedural writing (the water cycle, the scientific method)
- Concepts in character education/teambuilding (kindness, cooperation, sacrifice, loyalty)
- Different types/classifications in science/history/ geography (types of rocks, Native peoples, different ecosystems, types of resources/industries)
- Parts of a whole (parts of an insect, parts of the digestive system, parts of a castle)
- Prepare students to draw/paint/collage scenes in visual arts
- Illustrations of classroom rules/procedure

Sample Lessons

Remember: These lessons are only suggestions and can be used at any grade level with minor modifications!

Grades K-3

The Illustrator

This is a great way to start off the day and link in recalcitrant learners with that day's classroom activities and goals. It also makes neural connections fostering oral language in those students who need accelerated development.

Lesson Focus

To have students prepare for printing/writing by linking their experience and interest with classroom activities/curriculum and talking about it.

Activity

Level I

1. Students sit in a circle with one student (**"The Illustrator"**) standing in the middle (or in desks with one student at the front of the room)

2. Going to each seated student in turn, the teacher asks the child "What did you do last night?"

3. When the child responds ("I played soccer!") **The Illustrator** freezes in a still life of the activity.

4. The teacher asks the **The Illustrator** what he/she is doing and the child responds appropriately.

5. The teacher then asks **The Illustrator** how the activity can connect with something that has been studied in class. A possible response could be something like "A soccer ball is a sphere and we learned about spheres yesterday in math!" If the child cannot think of anything, another class member can volunteer and answer and, if correct, that child can become **The Illustrator**.

Level II

1. The Level I is repeated, but this time after the child in **The Illustrator** demonstrates the action, all of the children can stand up and copy the action of **The Illustrator.**

2. The teacher then asks: "What are you all doing?" and the children respond in unison. The teacher then asks: "Okay. Show me how this connects with something we have learned in our class."

3. Students individually freeze in a different still life representing what they think is a connection. The teacher taps in to various students and asks each one to describe what they are doing and why it is a connection.

Level III

1. Students play **The Illustrator** game in pairs:

    a. STUDENT A: (Sitting, pretending to look at something) "I watched a video last night."

    b. STUDENT B: (Crouching) "We watched a video in class about lions!" (Then freezing on hands and knees) "I played with my trucks last night."

    c. STUDENT A: "Trucks are one mode of transportation we learned about." (Holding a frozen position serving something) "My mom made us cookies Saturday!"

        ...and so on.

2. The teacher can circulate around helping those having problems or even freezing the group to look at a particularly good still life connection

Hints

•   The teacher can always suggest connections if the students are having trouble and then students can make a still life of the connection

•   Instead of asking children what they did last night, ask them about their favourite activity, food, animal— anything that will allow them to take their personal experience and kinesthetically link it to learning in the class.

Extension

Journals - Students can be asked to write about either what they did last night or the connections between what they do at home and what they do in school.

Grades 4-6

Event Flow

Sequencing events and understanding/predicting the changes that take place over a period of time are skills that are used in many curriculum areas. This still life application uses tapping in to help students process their understanding and give teachers a good tool to assess the level of that understanding.

Lesson Focus

To have students review and understand the main ideas and characters in a story or novel.

Activity

Level I

1. Place the students in groups of 4-5.
2. Using the still life technique, take a movie or book that everyone is familiar with and ask the groups to develop three Still Life pictures that illustrate the most important parts of the story. Give them only 4 minutes to complete this task!

3. Once the time is up, ask each group to display their Still Life and identify the parts of the story they have decided to show.

After the presentations are done, discuss the differences in what the groups chose as the "most important" in the piece chosen. Have the class vote on which Still Life pictures should be included as the **"Three Most Important Ideas"** in the movie or book chosen.

Level II

1. In their groups, have students look at a novel or story you are reading in class. Ask them to quickly develop the three most important ideas as *Still Life* pictures for that piece of literature and have them sequence the pictures in the order in which they occur.

2. Once groups are ready, have them display the first *Still Life*. Tap into the members of each group asking them questions about who they are in the story, how they feel, and what they think will happen.

3. Move on to the second and third *Still Life* images in the series, but this time, when *Tapping In*, make sure to focus on having them describe how they have changed as the story has progressed.

Level III

In their groups, students are to replay their *Still Life* pictures, with everyone becoming a different character with each run-through of the series.

4. Let them tap themselves in as they practice with the goal of coming up with a common group understanding of the main idea and event flow in the story.

5. Tell the groups you will be evaluating them and ask them to make sure they can give evidence to support their characters' points of view as they progress, as well as how they have physically represented the character within the still life. For example, the character who has gained courage should exhibit that courage in an understandable way to an observer by his or her body position.

Hints

•   It's important to ask the students to give oral evidence and rationale for the choices they make. For example, if a student representing a character who has developed courage in the story says when tapped in "I am now not afraid to try new things," make sure to ask why and have them give details to support their character's change. This is important for the kinesthetic learner in particular because even though they "know" the answer in their body, engaging their frontal lobe through metacognitive speaking helps to consolidate the neural connections surrounding that kinesthetic knowledge.

• Encouraging students to think about and make choices around how to physically represent their character's feelings, ideas, or development when using Still Life helps them better understand motivations, establishing new neural pathways that help them use that understanding better in speaking and writing tasks.

Extension

Writing - Have the students:

• write character sketches of the of the characters in the story or novel

• create plot graphs of the event flow

Grades 7-10

Living Diagram (science)

Students are asked to read and understand diagrams in many forms of writing and research. This exercise is excellent for helping them to understand what a diagram is and how it enhances text presentation. It also demonstrates how Still Life can be used to engage students in their own learning at the introduction of content.

Lesson Focus

To have students understand the parts of the cell and their functions.

Activity

Level II

(If students are not familiar with Still Life this can serve as a warm-up. If they are go directly to **LEVEL II***)*

1. In groups of 4-5, have students create a *Still Life* picture of a computer in a way that represents its most important parts in 90 seconds. Leave it up to them how to do it, but reinforce the rules of *Still Life* representation, i.e., being still without talking, different levels, facial expressions that somehow effectively portray their computer part.

2. When you say "freeze," make sure they can do it for 5 to 15 seconds.

3. Briefly use *Tapping In* to ask members of different groups what they are and why it is important to the computer.

4. Spend only a brief time on this and then move to **Level II**

Level II

1. Give students a list of the parts of a cell and their functions. It is best if this information does not include a diagram. Ask them to construct a *Still Life* picture in 3 to 4 minutes using the information given.

2. When they are ready, say "freeze" and use *Tapping In* to ask members of different groups what they are and why it is important to the cell.

3. Give them another few minutes and tell them everyone must be able to take the place of any part in the cell and the group *Still Life* should still look the same.

4. Ask the groups to change and *Tap In* randomly to assess their understanding.

Level III

1. Previous groups are given a blank diagram of a cell and asked to label it based on their understanding from their *Still Life*. Review these with the class after and have them correct any errors and answer any questions raised by the students.

2. Tell students to create a *Living Diagram* that represents the actual cell structure. When tapped in or pointed at, any part steps out for the diagram and describes:

    - What their formal name is (with spelling if desired!)
    - What their cell part does
    - Why their function is vital to the cell (or what would happen if the part failed)

3. Tell them that they will be assessed on the accuracy of their physical representation and oral descriptions and that they need to practice with each member playing

each part because you will decide randomly which representation to assess and so they must be ready.

4. Assess them either as they show their still life in front of the class or as each group comes up to your desk separately. In the latter case, the rest of the students could be working on an assignment as suggested in the **Extension** below.

Hints

*   **Level II** could easily be used as a quiz

*   Having them create their own diagram from the information *before* they see the actual diagram is extremely powerful because it triggers deeper thinking about cell structure and how it would make sense for a cell to be constituted. Once the brain is engaged like this, it is much easier to absorb the material related to the actual structure of the cell.

Extension

One-page Essay – Ask students to write a one-page essay entitled The Superior Cell: How I would change the cell structure to improve on nature's handiwork. Ask them to explain what parts they would change and why as well as including a diagram (which could be rendered with friends as a Still Life once the essay is complete).

CHAPTER 10

STRATEGY II
BACK AND FORTH

"That kid never shuts up in class, but now he's talking about what I want him to talk about and loving it. He's also much better behaved afterward."

—Grade 6 Teacher

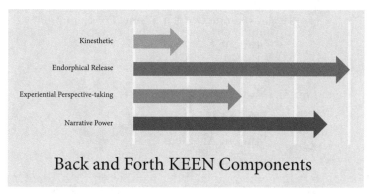

Back and Forth KEEN Components

Introduction

Don't let the simplicity of this strategy fool you. It is a quick and easy strategy that bears great fruit, particularly in fostering student engagement! It can be used with almost any material and played daily.

Why BACK AND FORTH helps struggling students

- It is *fun* and will have students playing as they work with your curriculum

- It improves predicting and connection-making skills

- It allows them to partner as they learn, exposing them to the complexities of oral language that they must attack as a team!

The Strategy Basics

1. Have the students in pairs or in groups of three.

2. Tell the students they have 1 to 2 minutes to tell the story of "Little Red Riding Hood" (a nursery rhyme or a movie that both partners are familiar with will also serve). When telling the story, however, each partner is only allowed one word at a time. For example:

    Student A: "Once"
    Student B: "upon"
    Student A: "a"
    Student B: "time"
    Student A: "there"
    Student B: "was..."

3. Model this structure if necessary with one student as a volunteer working with the teacher to show students how it should work.

4. Once they are familiar with *Back and Forth*, ask them to do it with curriculum material. Examples are given below.

KEEN Considerations

- Emphasize to the students that each person can only say one word and that initially students should not "put words" into each other's mouths. They must go with the flow.

- Pairs are ideal and groups of three will work, but once you get much larger than that, the exercise is exceedingly difficult to develop a coherent story because of all of the minds that must agree for it to work.

- Rehearsal of the *Back and Forth* stories is acceptable if your goal is to have students accurately recount specific information.

Variations that Deepen Learning

1. This strategy is an excellent review technique if you ask students to play Back and Forth together and then test their knowledge individually.

2. Ask curriculum questions of a pair of students who then must answer in Back and Forth format.

General Cross-curricular Applications

- Summarize narratives or parts of narratives

- Review information for quizzes, tests, or other culminating tasks

- Brainstorm what the students know about a topic at the beginning of a new unit, activating prior knowledge

- Help students with creative writing pieces, using the game as a brainstorming or pre-writing activity

- Help students review basic sentence structure, paragraph, and essay structure

- Retell and explain processes or procedures (e.g., orally explaining how to complete a math question, using all steps in the right order)

- Use in any situation where students are asked to orally respond to questions that can be processed first through the *Back and Forth* format

Sample Lessons

Remember: These lessons are only suggested and can be used at any grade level with minor modifications!

Grades K-3

First...Then...Finally

This helps combine the learning power of Back and Forth with practice in the important skills of sequencing and identifying the main ideas.

Lesson Focus

To have students sequence stories properly.

Activity

Level I

1. Have pairs of students play *Back and Forth* with a fairy tale or movie.

2. Ask them to take a book or story they have heard in class and render it in the following manner using *Back and Forth:*

    a. "First...(A sentence about what happened at the beginning of the story)"

    b. "Next...(A sentence about what happened in the middle of the story)"

    c. "Finally...(A sentence about what happened at the end of the story)"

Level II

Ask students to make up their own "First...Then...Finally" story using *Back and Forth*

Level III

Have students add "because" after each part of the story to give supporting details (i.e., "First...Abdul did not want to try pizza **because** he did not like cheese")

Hints

- If students want to rehearse to get it right, allow it.

- There may be some frustration in some pairs because one person is not saying what the other thinks she should say. This is a great opportunity to discuss empathy and the fact that different people think different ways.

Extension

Once they have a "First...Then...Finally" *Back and Forth* story that they can relate smoothly, ask them to write it down and it can become the basis for a *Still Life* or Brain-Writer story!

Grades 4-6

Ancient Civilizations

Back and Forth can be used to review content in any area of the curriculum and is used here to have students recall information about the life and times of various early human communities.

Lesson Focus

To have students review how ancient peoples on each of the seven continents shaped the environment to support their physical needs for food and housing.

Activity

Level I

1. Have pairs of students play *Back and Forth* as described above with a fairy tale or movie

2. Have students use *Back and Forth* to create a factual sentence about what the people on a particular continent did for food.

Level II

Split Personality

1. Have two volunteers who have practiced creating factual sentences for the topic in *Back and Forth* come to the front. They sit on chairs or stools back to back so they cannot see each other and the class can see them in profile.

2. They are then asked a question like "Describe why the Nile River was so important to early Egyptians." They must answer in *Back and Forth* fashion without looking at each other.

3. After they answer, ask the class to discuss how accurate and comprehensible their answers were.

4. Have the rest of the class practice the answer to the question and see if there are other volunteers who think they can answer better.

Level III

Multiple Personalities

Play Split Personality with four people who are in a circle and must answer the curriculum questions—one word at a time in sequence.

Hints

- When playing *Split/Multiple Personality*, the activity can be facilitated by coming up with a set of questions about the material and then giving them to the pairs to practice first.

Extension

See if the class as a whole can come up with a Back and Forth summary that would give one fact about food and housing for the peoples on each of the seven continents.

Grades 7-10

Novel Study (English)

As part of reading and understanding a novel, students are often asked to examine the plot, describe characters and their motivations, and identify the style(s) of writing used. Back and Forth *is a great alternate activity to add to teacher lecturing and class discussion because it reinforces the learning that takes place in other approaches and hooks in those who may not have been as engaged previously.*

Lesson Focus

Reviewing various characteristics of a novel under study.

Activity

Level I

1. Have pairs of students play *Back and Forth* as described above with a fairy tale or movie.

2. Have students use *Back and Forth* to create a single-sentence description of each character that highlights their most telling feature of their personality.

Level II

Have students use Back and Forth to describe the four sentences—each in a different style—that are accurate about the novel. The styles are:

- Narrative
- Expository
- Descriptive
- Persuasive/Argumentative

Once the sentences are complete, have the students share them (in *Back and Forth* format) and discuss whether they are both accurate and written in the correct style.

Level III

Have students use *Back and Forth* to create a sentence for each of the elements of plot as they are revealed in the novel:

- Exposition
- Rising Action
- Climax
- Falling action
- Resolution

When they are ready, allow students to share with other pairs or in front of the class.

Hint

- Make sure to use a time frame so the students stay focused (i.e., "You must have your plot element sentences ready in 10 minutes!"

Extension

After practicing these in Back and Forth format with a partner, assess students by having them complete the tasks in Levels I through III on their own. Having practiced with another in this fashion, they should find the task easier and achieve higher when they are on their own—and don't have to worry about the other person's mind getting in the way!

CHAPTER 11

STRATEGY III
BRAIN-WRITER

"See that girl—she hates those boys. But look at her now: she's leading them and they're following. She's empowered."

The teacher pointed to a small group in her Grade 1 class who were using a KEEN activity to create a story. She explained that the reason the girl disliked the boys was because of how rough they were on the playground, often pushing her and taking her toys. In previous classroom groups, she was quiet and withdrawn. But today, she was calling the shots, smiling and obviously reveling in her ability to have the boys willingly be the visual images in her story.

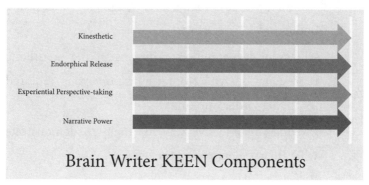

Kinesthetic

Endorphical Release

Experiential Perspective-taking

Narrative Power

Brain Writer KEEN Components

Introduction

This is one of the most powerful KEEN strategies. It leverages tremendous engagement and cognition and can be applied in many different contexts. In this cooperative small-group activity, one person in the group is the *Writer* and pretends to type at a keyboard while narrating a story. Other students in the group are *"Mental Images"* who bring the story to life. The students will need some open areas in the classroom for this activity, although these can just be spaces small enough for 4-5 students to sit in chairs or on the floor near their desks.

Why BRAIN-WRITER helps struggling students

- Permits movement while still connected to the curriculum
- Helps them create a narrative around curriculum material that both engages them with the material and creates meaning, giving the students personal ownership of the material and how they learn it
- Allows boys to process oral language while using bodies
- Allows for deeper understanding by linking kinesthetic representation with frontal lobe processing required for higher-order thinking
- Provides an effective way for them to demonstrate what they understand to the teacher

- Gives them motivation to learn from other members of the group

The Strategy Basics

1. The *Writer* sits in a chair; others in the group remain sitting or crouching near the *Writer* and only stand up and move when they are pointed into life. So the *Writer* might say, "Once there was a sun shining in the solar system" and then point to a student in the group who becomes the writer's *mental image by standing* and miming a shining sun.

2. Only the *Writer* or the assigned *mental image* speaks when prompted to (e.g., the *Writer* narrates, "The traveller said, 'Leave me alone!," and the character would repeat exactly what the *Writer* has just said).

3. Fast movements and action sequences are to be performed in slow motion.

4. The *Writer* must get everyone in each group is involved—even if some people are inanimate objects, and if people have to take on two or more roles.

KEEN Considerations

- As was suggested with *Still Life*, when introducing *Brain-Writer*, it is sometimes good to allow students to start by using a familiar movie or fairy tale. Have them do it briefly and make sure they are following the rules (e.g., only the *Writer* speaks, everyone is involved, slo-mo used to illustrate action sequences, etc.).

- Keep stories short: 2-4 minutes long

- The students should know and understand what the teacher wants them to learn/display as a result of the activity (e.g., "Your *Brain-Writer* story must name the organs in the digestive system and demonstrate what each does.") An initial *Brain-Writer* story may be modelled with students by the teacher as the Writer so that the students are aware of the expectations. Emphasize that the *Brain-Writer* stories will be assessed for how they display learning, not acting ability!

- *Brain-Writer* is an excellent assessment tool (See Grades 7-10 example below)

Variations that Deepen Learning

1. Once the *Brain-Writer* story is played, change the person who is the *Writer*. Have every person in the group rotate through the *Writer* role so that every person can demonstrate knowledge of the material, and every person has tried each of the roles.

2. The author could also be rotated within the story as a new Writer continues the story from the point where the previous Writer ended. The goal here is to keep everyone engaged with the story and make sure that even when four to five authors participate to tell one

2-minute story, the whole story is sequenced correctly, flows, and makes sense.

General Cross-curricular Applications

- Demonstrate understanding of procedures in science, being able to name and describe the procedure step by step (mitosis, the scientific method, how natural resources are harvested)

- Depict systems in science (body systems, weather systems)

- Summarize entire stories/narratives, or parts of stories; avoid having the students read directly from a text

- Summarize events in history and geography (Rebellions of 1837, causes of World War I, formation of landforms, etc.)

- Describe how parts of a whole work (the parts of the cell, the different parts of the government)

- Weave different related concepts into a narrative that help students understand the concepts (themes in English literature, dependent/independent variable in science, etc.)

Sample Lessons

Remember: These lessons are only suggested and can be used at any grade level with minor modifications!

Grades K-3

Story Time

Children of all ages love to have stories read to them, and it is a staple in their early years of school. It helps children emotionally connect with books and engages them in narrative, a form of learning and communication that has been hardwired into the brain over centuries to our most primitive form of learning and communication. However, there are students who can stop paying attention or be disruptive during this time because the story is not interesting to them or they don't understand because the vocabulary is too difficult—or they think they have a better story in their heads! Adapting Brain-Writer for use during this time can be helpful for both teacher and students.

Lesson Focus

To have students become more deeply engaged in the story read to them and be able to make connections between the story and their own experiences.

Activity

Level I

1. With students sitting as they usually do during story time, the teacher begins to read from a book, telling the students he will need some mental images to make the

book come to life and will choose those images from the students who appear to be listening really well.

2. After reading a line, the teacher points to a student and they come to the front and illustrate what has been read. Encourage students to represent with their bodies and facial expressions the feeling evoked by the reading (i.e., when the teacher reads, "Jason hated having to put on his mittens to go out and play in the snow," the child representing Jason can mime putting on the gloves with a sour face).

3. Feel free to have a number of children come up and play a main character during the reading, but also remember that someone could also be the mittens, for example!

Level II

1. Once the story has been read to the students, have them work in pairs or small groups to retell the story, with one student as the *Writer* (or *"Teller"*) and the other(s) being the mental images.

2. If there are multiple copies of the story, the *Writer* in each group could be reading from it (or pretending to in the case of non-readers)

3. If desired, different groups could come up and present their story with the writer taking the teacher's chair to tell the story.

Level III

1. Have students use Brain-Writer to create a story like the one used in the previous levels. The only criterion is that they have to be able to explain how it is like the previous story. This will allow for a differentiation between students ranging from a story where the participants hate putting on mittens (the only difference is that it is the classroom student and not Jason in the story) to exotic connections where perhaps a student moves to Florida so they don't have to play in the snow! The important part here can come when students watch other groups' *Brain-Writer* stories and the teacher reinforces through discussion the connections that have been made; then students can immediately be asked to do another Brain-Writer story that makes more complex connections.

2. Another *Brain-Writer* task could be to use the same characters and setting but tell a different story.

Hints

*   Allowing students to discuss in their groups how they will represent their story can give hints to the *Writer* and also help students practice oral language skills.

*   Remember to rotate the author with each new level of group work.

Extension

Writing - Students can be asked to take the stories they have retold and/or created and write them out. Or they could be told that if they wrote a story/paragraph/sentence, they could choose some friends to render it in *Brain-Writer* fashion.

Grades 4-6

The Digestive System (Science)

The ability to understand parts of a whole and how they function together to create the whole is an important skill for students in many curriculum areas. Using Brain-Writer to help students understand parts and processes can help students generate engagement and cognition by generating a meaningful connection between themselves and the curriculum.

Lesson Focus

To have students be able to name the five main organs of the digestive system and describe their functions.

Activity

Level I

1. If students are not familiar with *Brain-Writer* have them practice it briefly with a well-known movie or fairy tale.

2. Once they have demonstrated an understanding of the strategy, have them use it to describe the parts of the digestive system. Be clear about what they need to be able to demonstrate with their stories.

3. After 5 minutes, do an interim assessment, either privately as you circulate around or having each group demonstrate their *Brain-Writer* stories for the class. Correct misperceptions and inaccuracies.

Level II

1. Students are asked to develop a consistent 2 to 4 minute description of the passage of food through the digestive system that can be told by *anyone* in the group.

2. Have one group observe another's story and critique it for accuracy in representation.

Level III

Ask students to create a *Brain-Writer* story that demonstrates what happens when organs are mistreated or fail due to disease, etc.

Hints

- Allow the students to create stories that are from any genre they like. For example, one group may describe the process from the perspective of the food moving through the system in which the food describes how it feels as it journeys. Another group might choose a dispassionate third-person description that reads like a textbook. The students' choice of style is important for giving them ownership of the material.

- Humour is acceptable if it does not result in inaccuracy in relation to the curriculum material. Telling students to make sure that the presentations are "suitable for family viewing" will discourage crudeness.

- Make sure to ask students to account for their choices in portraying parts of the system and to ask them to be as accurate as possible in their representations. For example, a student bobbing his head up and down while portraying the esophagus is not as accurate as one who uses his hands to mimic the muscle contractions that make the food move through the passageway.

- Discussion between students is important, especially when you rotate through different *Writers*. However, give the groups deadlines so that they stay focused on finding solutions to the task at hand.

Extension

- After having the students create Brain-Writer stories where each person has been the Writer, ask students to write an essay that describes the major organs of the digestive system and their roles. They should be able to do this more easily than if they had just been told about the digestive system.

- Ask the groups to come up with a new organ, put it into their digestive system, explain how it works, and justify why it is needed.

Grades 7-10

Assessing Understanding (History/Native Studies)

Here is a description of how Brain-Writer can be used as an assessment tool for authentic assessment. It can be used on its own or in combination with a written test or assignment.

Lesson Focus

To assess the level of knowledge and understanding students have at the end of a unit about the different groups of aboriginal peoples in Canada and the differences and similarities in their cultures and worldviews.

Activity

1. If students are not familiar with Brain-Writer, have them practice it briefly with a well-known movie or fairy tale.

2. Once they have demonstrated an understanding of the strategy, tell them you are going to have them demonstrate to you their understanding of aboriginal peoples using Brain-Writer.

3. Circulate through the different groups and assess each group on the accuracy of the content demonstrated. Give reasons why the group has received the mark (formative assessment). Avoid having the students perform their stories in front of the class; more introverted students will not feel "put on the spot." This also discourages the groups from focusing on making the story funny, as opposed to demonstrating knowledge. However, feel free to point out to the class when a group is demonstrating that knowledge.

4. Once assessed, give the groups the opportunity to work on improving their stories. Tell them that for the summative assessment you will be able to choose any member of the group as the *Writer*; this will require them to practice it numerous times with the different members of the group as *telling the story*. This reduces the cognitive diversity within the group by encouraging the students who understand to help those who don't.

5. When they are ready, have each group come to you and present their Brain-Writer stories. The teacher can ask questions, rotate the *Writers* if desired, and then give the group a summative evaluation.

Hints

- Students in this age group will often try and "be funny" in their stories because humour appeals to them and their rapidly developing higher-order thinking skills.

They also like to use it to impress their peers. As we have seen, having fun is extremely important for engagement purposes for some students and should be permitted. However, the assessment is on their knowledge and skills and they need to know that they will not do well if they do not represent the necessary information accurately—no matter how "entertaining" their *Brain-Writer* story. This is where the formative assessment described in #3 earlier is so important. Saying, "Well, boys, that was enjoyable, but not historically accurate and would only rate a 35% right now," is often exactly what is needed to get their competitive juices flowing and have them prove that they are both clever and smart.

- It is often helpful to give groups a bit of extra time, if possible, to perfect their presentations for their summative assessment. It is surprising how this activity can take struggling students and have them want to do well since they feel mastery is attainable within the *Brain-Writer* approach.

Extension

Groups that do well on the summative assessment can be asked to present their *Brain-Writer* stories to the class to highlight what good work looks like or to review for a written assessment on the same material.

CHAPTER 12

STRATEGY IV

HANDY MEMORY

"They got 95% on the test and it was still 88% a week later. It only took 15 minutes to teach the concepts. I figured teaching it would take at least two more classes! But we did it in one day and they loved it!"
—High school teacher commenting on her students learning in earth science after a KEEN activity.

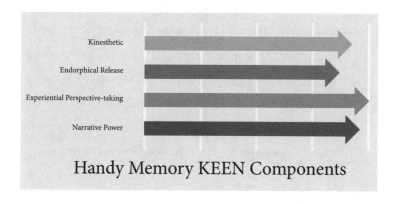

Handy Memory KEEN Components

Introduction

This is a simple strategy that can bear great fruit in terms of engagement and memory, particularly for kinesthetic learners. It allows them to create a bodily link to curriculum while still sitting in their desks and can be used by the teacher to help students remember terms, processes, and concepts.

Why HANDY MEMORY Helps Struggling Students

- Permits movement while still connected to the curriculum
- Links language memory to movement
- Allows them control over the curriculum as they create a symbolic narrative and process material from different perspectives

The Strategy Basics

Take the material you wish to have the students learn or review and link it to a hand movement. Here is an example:

1. Introduce the word by writing it on the board. Provide its definition (e.g., cytoplasm – the jelly-like substance that fills the cell). Use your hands to illustrate the meaning in a way that makes sense to you (i.e., you may rub your fingers together or pretend to be pulling apart a sticky material) and ask students to mimic your movement.

2. Say "cytoplasm" as you do the actions and have the students repeat it doing the same thing.

3. Repeat the word/action with the students five times.

4. Continue discussion on the topic, but periodically complete the action for them and ask them what it means.

KEEN Considerations

- It's easier to start by using one hand until students get the knack of it, but two hands are good for complicated words or concepts.

- Some students may not feel they need to do the hand movements to retain the information. That's okay because their learning style may be more auditory or visual, but it can be a lifesaver in terms of cognition for other students. The activity is fun, particularly in the variations that follow, so most students really enjoy it.

- If students create the hand movements on their own, it's important for the teacher to make sure they are accurate enough to represent the material. However, remember, if it allows students to access the material in a way that increases their engagement and retention, it doesn't have to resonate with the teacher or other students—it is differentiated learning in its truest sense!

Variations That Deepen Learning

1. Students can work on their own or in pairs to come up with their own hand movements related to the

material. This can be powerful because they have to do the cognitive work of creating the movement. This can also lead to good questioning by the teacher and discussion that helps the teacher to understand the students' thinking and forces the students to think metacognitively about why they created the hand movement and what it means to them.

2. *Silent Review* – Alone or in groups, ask students to develop a sequence of hand movements that represents vocabulary (*types of angles*), concepts (*roles in medieval society*), or processes (*steps in the scientific method*). They can then show these to others and have them guess what is being represented and verify that it is, indeed, correct. Students can also be asked to justify the hand movement created and prove that it is a logical representation of the curriculum material.

General Cross-curricular Applications

- Represent vocabulary being studied in language, science, history, geography, or math
- Steps or procedures in science or in procedural writing (the water cycle, the scientific method)
- Concepts in character education/teambuilding (kindness, cooperation, sacrifice, loyalty)
- Different types/classifications in science/history/ geography (types of rocks, Native peoples, different ecosystems, types of resources/industries)

1. Parts of a whole (parts of an insect, parts of the digestive system, parts of a castle)

2. Illustrations of classroom rules/procedures

Sample Lessons

Remember: These lessons are only suggested and can be used at any grade level with minor modifications!

Grades K-3

Handy Spelling

Helping young children to review and remember letters and spelling is an easy use of this technique. It can be done for a few minutes every day and will be popular, especially with the boys. Since they lag in oral language development, this can help them use their well-developed kinesthetic-spatial abilities in the service of the curriculum and more efficient oral language development.

Lesson Focus

To have students review spelling and simple vocabulary.

Activity

Level I

1. Over the course of a few days, the teacher develops common hand movements to illustrate each letter in

the alphabet with the students. Five to six new letters a day works well, with review of the previous letters at the end. It is important in this case that everyone has the same hand movement for each letter.

2. Make sure to have students say the letter as they complete the movements.

3. When finished, the students should be able to say or sing their ABCs with the movements as they do so.

Level II

1. The teacher then uses the letter-hand movements to have students spell out words, saying the letters as the movements are made.

2. Words are then spelled out only in movements and students have to guess what word is being spelled out and spell that word after correctly guessing.

3. Students are invited up to spell out words with their hands and have others guess the word. If a student correctly guesses and is able to spell it back, then they can come up and sign a new word for the group.

Level III

1. Students play Handy Spelling in pairs.

   i. Student A has the written text of a word and asks the other to spell it. Student B does so using hands and spelling it out loud.

   ii. If correct, Student B now quizzes the Student A on

a new word from the list.

iii. If incorrect, Student A must spell it correctly using hands and words and Student B must copy it. Student A continues until Student B gets a word correct. Then they switch.

2. Ask students to make up their own games using Handy Spelling and share them with the class.

Hints

- Because struggling learners at this age usually have poorly developed fine motor skills, avoid making the hand movements too intricate; simple is better.

- Leveraging this for writing can be accomplished by telling students that if they write a sentence they can then communicate it using their handy memory. Often, unwilling writers need the kinesthetic reward at the end of the task to get them over their writer's block!

Extension

Spelling Sentences – Allow a struggling student who is particularly "handy" with this strategy to review for a spelling test by spelling out sentences with his or her hands, which the class then has to write down.

Grades 4-6

The Punctuator

This Handy Memory approach can often add zing to the curriculum areas that focus on grammar and sentence structure. Because these concepts are so far removed from the everyday usage of language—particularly those who do poorly in school— these strategies provide a fun experiential pathway to both engagement and cognition.

Lesson Focus

To have students understand and remember the different basic punctuation marks and their roles.

Activity

LEVEL I

1.   Teach the students the following:

Punctuation Mark	Handy Movement	Sound (Optional)
Capitalization	Both Hands in the Air	Breathing "Hah"
Period	Stop gesture	Tire skid sound "Rrrrr"
Comma	Arms crossed	Heavy Sigh "Ahhh..."
Question Mark	Curled arm above head	" mmmMM?"
Exclamation Mark	Fist straight in the air	"Whoo-Hoo!"
Colon	Drum beat	"Dum – Dum!"
Quotation Mark (Open)	Two fingers twitch left	Squeaky "OOH-ooh"
Quotation Mark (Closed)	Two fingers twitch right	Squeaky "ooh-OOH"

2. Write a sentence on the board and have them practice with you using the Punctuator sounds/movements

Level II

1. Once the students understand what to do, put them in pairs and practice reading sentences from a book that is regularly used in class or one that they are reading in language arts.

2. Once they are successful at this, ask them to write a sentence with proper punctuation and have their partner be the Punctuator. Then have them switch back and forth until they feel they can do it with ease.

Level III

Stand and deliver – Hot seat where one person has to do all of the correct actions.

Grades 7-10

BEDMAS (Math)

Math has any number of formulas and procedures that students must remember and use. The acronym BEDMAS is used to describe the order of operations a student must use to solve problems requiring multiple operations. It is a mnemonic device that helps students remember to do their work in the following order: Brackets, Exponents, Division, Multiplication, Addition, and Subtraction. Adding Handy

Memory to the mix helps trigger better recall for those who are more kinesthetic.

Lesson Focus

To remember BEDMAS quickly and easily.

Activity

Level I

As the teacher, you can create a hand movement for each of the steps in BEDMAS and have students copy them while saying the name of the step.

Level II

1. Ask students to work in pairs and create their own handy memory signs for each step. Tell them they must be able to justify logically why they have chosen the hand movements they did.

2. When they have created them, have them show them to other groups of students

Hint

- Before teaching future formulas, introduce students to them by having them find the definition in the math text, create Handy Memory signs, and then discuss what they chose and why. This will greatly increase their engagement and cognition when you teach them to apply the formula.

Extension

Have a contest where students are asked to create hand movements as representations of formulas/processes/rules, etc. they have learned in math previously. Volunteers can be chosen to demonstrate the movement and others in the class have to guess what is being represented. This is a great activity as part of a unit review!

CHAPTER 13

STRATEGY V
3-Way Conversation

"Did you hear what he just said!?"

A school principal talking to the classroom teacher after Jamal, who was usually seated by himself away from the rest of the class because of his behaviour and lack of engagement, poked a friend in his group using a KEEN activity for geography task and demanded *"Get serious— we only have 5 minutes to get this done."*

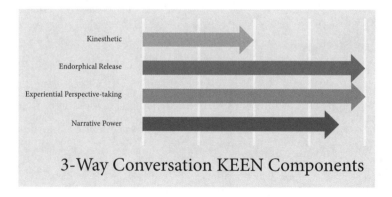

3-Way Conversation KEEN Components

Introduction

This strategy leverages the social nature of students to playfully help them focus their minds on not one but two curriculum areas! The fact that the brain has to work harder to successfully participate in 3-Way Conversation makes the activity a challenge that can be used by the teacher to reinforce curriculum skills and content.

Why 3-WAY CONVERSATION Helps Struggling Students

- It is *fun* and will have students playing as they work with your curriculum

- It provides a challenging task in the form of a game that allows them to develop their oral language in a non-threatening fashion.

- It focuses on developing effective questions that require more use of the frontal lobes and higher-order thinking

- It lets them change positions physically during the activity

The Strategy Basics

1. Ask the students to get into groups of three, sitting side by side as if they were on an airplane. The person in the middle is the *responder* and the ones on either side are the questioners.

2. At your signal, a 3-minute round begins. The questioner on the left asks the *responder* a question about a specific topic (i.e., "What's your favourite food?"). The *responder* must turn toward the questioner and answer immediately.

3. A soon as the *responder* has responded, the questioner on the right asks a question about a different topic (i.e. "How many people do you have in your family?"), and the *responder* must quickly turn to that questioner and answer.

4. The game continues back and forth with each questioner on the outside asking in turn questions about their topic and the *responder* turning to answer them. The round ends when:

    - A questioner on either side wins because *responder* cannot respond to a question within a few seconds,

        or

    - The *responder* wins because a questioner cannot come up with a question within a few seconds of the *responder's* last response

        or

    - Time runs out before the *responder* can be stumped.

5. Have students switch places after each round so that everyone gets to be the *responder*.

6. Once students are familiar with the game, the teacher can designate the question topics (i.e., the questioner

on one side can ask about what was learned in science that day and the other can ask questions about the novel being studied in class!)

KEEN Considerations

- It is often good when students first start to play the game to set a firm 3- to 5-second limit for the person in the middle to answer questions so that the game moves along.
- Younger students may need more time.
- At the beginning the answer must just be possible and reasonable, but when you move into curriculum areas, the answers need to be more accurate.

Variations that Deepen Learning

1. Discuss with students the nature of their questions, asking them to reflect on:
   - the types of questions that are easiest to answer and why
   - the types of questions that would make it harder for the *responder* to answer
   - why it is beneficial for the questioners to ask questions that involve explanation, description, or justification

   Help the students understand that "thick" questions involving more detailed thought and information will be more difficult for the *responder*, requiring him/her to think harder than to answer with "yes" or "no" to questions.

2. Have both questioners ask questions about different aspects of a single topic or curriculum area.

3. Allow students to prepare questions on curriculum topics and bring them to their questioner's chair.

General Cross-curricular Applications

- Reviewing for tests/quizzes
- Finding out what students know about a topic at the beginning of a new unit, activating prior knowledge
- Developing deeper, better questioning ability in students
- Fostering deeper understanding in any curriculum area
- Helping students review basic sentence structure, paragraph, and essay structure

Sample Lessons

Remember: These lessons are only suggested and can be used at any grade level with minor modifications!

Grades K-3

Community TV Reporter

The extra kinesthetic in this variation of 3-Way Conversation seems to really help younger students ease into the activity and get the most out of it.

Lesson Focus

To help students come up with questions and answers about people in their community.

Activity

Level I

1. Seat students in pairs. Give each of them a paper towel tube, magic marker (with cap on!), or other prop that they can pretend is a microphone.

2. Ask them to take turns asking each other questions about what they did last night or at recess. The only rule is that a person can only speak when they are speaking into the microphone.

3. Once they are used to this, have them sit down. Place three chairs at the front of the room facing the class.

4. Choose a volunteer to be the *responder* and sit in the middle chair (without a microphone). Tell the students the *responder* is a firefighter and they will be reporters invited to ask questions. Allow other students to come and sit with their microphones and alternately ask one question of the firefighter. Once they ask their question they can return to their place in the class.

After a suitable time, switch *responders* and make them other important people in the community or world.

Level II

1. Students can work in threes, with the two sitting on the outside each using their microphones to ask questions.

2. The teacher is timer. After a couple of minutes the teacher says "freeze" and "switch." Everyone changes places so that everyone eventually gets to be the responder.

Level III

The students can play *3-Way Conversation* as described in the "Strategy Basics" section earlier.

Hints

- Some students may need to be prompted and helped with questions initially; as they see the teacher and other students modelling questions, they should find it easier to come up with their own.

- A list of general questions on the board or on a sheet distributed to students can also help them feel confident asking questions.

Extension

Students can develop questions for important people in their school community (janitor, secretary, principal, librarian, etc.) and these people can be invited to be the *responder* in the hot seat!

Grades 4-6

Daily Delivery (Multiple curriculum areas)

This approach to 3-Way Conversation can be used to create a fun daily review that has students heading out the door with their minds full of what you have taught them that day. Its game-show approach is also surprisingly effective in helping struggling students pay attention throughout the day.

Lesson Focus

To have students review the daily learning in the last 15 minutes of the day before leaving for home.

Activity

Level I

1. Have students familiar with the *3-Way Conversation* format play the game with their own topics.

2. Then ask them to play the game using only topics from the curriculum being studied in class.

Level II

1. Once students are familiar with using 3-Way Conversation with the curriculum, start each day by

reminding them that you will be looking for three good questions about each subject area that is covered in class that day. Preference will be given to those students who have good "thick" questions.

2. In the last 15 minutes, once everything is ready for departure, tell the students it is *Daily Delivery* time and allow them to take out their questions, form small *3-Way Conversation* groups, and play the game using questions they have created during the day

3. After 5 to 7 minutes, allow volunteers to come to the front and play a fast-paced version of *3-Way Conversation* where pauses and mistakes cause the participant to lose their place in the chair and be replaced by someone else. The goal is to be in one of the three chairs when the bell rings.

Level III

Once a month there could be a Jeopardy-like *Daily Delivery* at lunch time in the gym or library where the questions have to be from the previous month's learning and the champions from the weeks before can strut their stuff!

Hints

• Initially, you may want to leave a few minutes at the end of each subject period to help students consider questions that might be used in the *Daily Delivery*.

- Some students might not write down questions, but I would allow them to participate anyway. It may be maddening, but I have found some of the "laziest" students about writing can come up with extremely effective questions and answers in the spur of the moment that reveal a good understanding of material I thought they were not paying attention to. Remember, engagement is the first prerequisite for learning and if they are engaged without the notes, so be it.

Extension

Daily Delivery questions can be collected by the teacher with the understanding that the best of them will be used as quizzes/tests for the curriculum material in question.

Grades 7-10

On the Hot Seat! (English, History, Civics)

This approach to 3-Way Conversation is excellent for helping students gain a better understanding for the motivations and life-experience of historical figures or fictional characters. The responder *has to get inside the head of another person and respond with answers that are either accurate according to the historical record or source or plausible because of the nature of the individual being portrayed.*

Lesson Focus

Understanding historical or literary figures.

Activity

Level I

1. Have students familiar with the *3-Way Conversation* format play the game with their own topics.

2. Then ask them to play the game using only topics from the curriculum being studied in class.

Level II

1. The teacher selects an area of focus (e.g., novel, historical period, current issue) and asks the students to focus on a person/character related to the area and write down five questions that the person in question should be able to answer.

2. The students move into groups of four: Three *3-Way Conversation* players and a *referee* who decides if an answer is acceptable by referring to the text/novel/teacher. Everyone rotates at three 3-minute intervals and takes turns as the *responder, questioner,* and *referee.*

3. After practicing like this, each group can send a representative to sit in the hot seat competing with other groups from the class.

Level III

Set up the 3-Way Conversation so that the *responder* has to be one person for the person on the right (e.g., Pretty Boy from *The Outsiders*) and another for the person on the left (General Montcalm). This can be very challenging and even confusing, but if students have come up with good questions it requires a very high level of thinking to successfully stay in the *responder's* hot seat!

Hints

- The *responder* does not have to "act" like the character/historical figure. It is not theatre. They just have to answer with the same logic and reasoning that the person in question would.

- The questions directed at the responder should deal with thoughts, feelings, and motivations for actions that occurred in the historical record or novel. Questions like the following are most useful:
  - Why did you act/react the way you did when…?
  - How has your relationship changed with…?
  - How might your experience be different if…?
  - How did you feel when…?

Extension

After being in the hot seat, students should be able to approach "writing in character" with much more accuracy and engagement, as they have had to put themselves in the mind of someone else and answer questions as that person.

CHAPTER 14

STRATEGY VI
CONNECT SCENES

"Please let us stay! I know we need the extra help, but I don't like feeling dumb. When we do it like this, I feel like I'm as good as any other kid in the class."

—Abeela, Grade 7 special education student on being asked to leave a KEEN activity for her daily remedial session

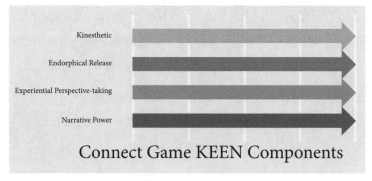

Kinesthetic

Endorphical Release

Experiential Perspective-taking

Narrative Power

Connect Game KEEN Components

Introduction

This last one is a bit more complex than the others but, when used correctly, it also provides the highest levels of engagement, cognition, and metacognition found among the

KEEN strategies. *Connect Scenes* provide a way to synthesize knowledge and develop deeper abilities to make connections, to inference, and to demonstrate learning transference by applying skills and concepts in a variety of areas. The activity is best introduced once students are familiar with *Still Life* and *Brain-Writer*, since the skills learned in those strategies are also useful in *Connect Scenes*.

Because the strategy has a number of distinct, sequential steps that develop skills to use it effectively, the Strategy Basics section will be very detailed and ask you to teach the strategy for a bit of time each day over a few weeks. I promise that if you take the time to do it as I suggest, you will be completely *amazed* at how powerful it will be for teaching and learning in your class. If you've come this far with me, you understand intuitively the power that is contained in these activities, so why not give it a try? You won't regret it!

Why CONNECT SCENES Help Struggling Students

- It helps link curricula with their strongest areas of brain function, which often involve a "kinesthetic intuition" that serves them well on the sports field, but less frequently in class where using this intuition is labeled "impulsive" or disruptive in class.

- Helps them create a narrative around a curriculum material that both engages them with the material and creates meaning, giving the students personal ownership of the material and how they learn it.

- Allows them to process oral language while using bodies.

- Allows for deeper understanding by linking kinesthetic representation with frontal lobe processing required for higher-order thinking.

- Effective for authentic assessment of understanding that is not pencil/paper.

- Gives them motivation to contribute as a "team player" in areas of classroom learning and curriculum.

The Strategy Basics

Understanding a Connect Scene (One 15 to 20 minute session)

1. Invite two extroverts to the front of the class.

2. Ask one to sit in chair and the other to stand behind the chair

3. When you give the signal, the student standing will walk around to the front of the chair and speak to the person sitting, saying the following, depending on the ages of children in the class:

   (Gr K-3) *"Hey, look at the new toy I got. Want to play?"*
   (Gr 4-6) *"Your brother says you took his bike without permission and broke it..."*
   (Gr 7-10) *"I wanted to thank you for trying out; I know you worked really hard, but I'm not going to be able to keep you on the team..."*

4. The person sitting is to go along with the scene, responding as a normal person would in that situation (i.e., the kids would pretend to play with the toy, the child might defend or explain about the bike, and the athlete might ask for some explanation or plead the case for staying on the team).

5. Only let the scene go on for 5 to 10 seconds and then say "freeze." The two should freeze immediately like when one pauses a video or DVD, keeping their body positions suspended in mid-conversation.

6. Now ask the rest of the class to look at the two as if they were in a photograph. If you just looked at the picture, what might be going on? Many students will say it is exactly what they just saw acted out, but ask them to look closer and forget what happened before. You may need to prompt them; for example, if one student has his hands above his head, you might say, "It looks like one person is describing to the other the size of the fish he caught."

7. Once you have a number of suggestions, take one and ask the person who did not start the last scene to start a new one by saying something that will get it going. So if you chose the scene with a fish story, then the person starting the scene could look at his/her outstretched hands and say, "Look at the size of this catfish I caught!" When the two are ready, say "connect!" The scene continues on from there.

8. Continue like this, freezing the participants after 5 to 10 seconds and having the students in the Connect Scene alternately start new scenes based on suggestions from the class once they hear you say "connect!"

KEEN Considerations for Understanding CONNECT SCENES

- Each Connect Scene must start from the frozen position that ended the previous scene and should make sense from those body positions. So it would make sense for two students who were crouched on the ground playing trucks to start a new scene where they are runners waiting for the starting gun, but it would not make sense to have them hanging from a cliff at the beginning of the new scene because their body positions were not stretched out enough at the end of the last scene to portray this at the beginning of the new scene.

- Participants must always cooperate and say "yes" to keep the scene going. So if one student says to another in scene, "Let's go fishing!" the other cannot say "No," but must help move the scene along by saying something like, "Great, I've got my fishing rod right here!"

- Participants in Connect Scenes must mime what they're pretending to do (i.e., after agreeing to go fishing the two must pretend to fish)

- Travelling, running, etc. are all done in slow motion and in the place where the scene is played (i.e., to run a race, participants pretend to run in place and do not move from the Connect Scene area).

Practicing Connect Scenes (A few minutes each day for a week)

1. Once students understand the concept, let them pair up and practice. Start with the same scene starter that was used in #3 . After 5 to 10 seconds say "freeze." Allow them 5 to 10 more seconds to decide together what their next Connect Scene will be by whispering to each other but not changing their body positions. After the allotted time, say "connect!" and the scene should begin.

2. Once students feel comfortable with doing the Connect Scenes like this, challenge them not to talk between Freeze and Connect, but to be ready to go with whatever scene is suggested by the first words spoken by the student who is supposed to start the scene.

KEEN Considerations When Practicing CONNECT SCENES

- Some teachers prefer using a bell or flicking the lights to signal students to freeze. That is fine at this point.

- As far as possible, allow students to partner with friends or people they are comfortable with. It is important for the success of this strategy that they feel safe to take risks in coming up with Connect Scenes.

- If partners seem to be having trouble, you could always include a suggestion after they freeze each time. Some possibilities are:

  - *A person walking his dog*
  - *Two elderly people out for a stroll*
  - *Someone giving directions to a lost person*
  - *A teacher helping a student with homework*
  - *Someone helping a friend look for a lost contact lens*
  - *Two ants talking about their adventures*
  - *A person meeting his shadow*
  - *A brother asking his sister not to tell he broke the vase*
  - *Kids playing in the sandbox*
  - *A waiter taking an order*
  - *Two cartoon characters*
  - *A person getting a driver's lesson*
  - *A child late for school being woken by a pare*nt

  As you can see, the suggestions range from the mundane to the fantastical; it really doesn't matter what scene they change to, only that the scene changes and that they make a connection to the previous scene through their body position.

- The scenes that the students create do not have to be entertaining to an observer. Remember, this is not acting. Do not show off "good" scenes at this point; it was necessary for demonstration purposes at the beginning, but no longer. If you do, you risk losing a great deal of benefit from the activity because it will turn off the introverts and cause the extroverts (many of whom already struggle in the classroom work) to try and be funny rather than keep the scenes going. The only criteria for success at this point is that pairs of students can move smoothly from one Connect Scene to another, getting better over time at coming up with ideas and keeping the scenes going for 10 to 15 seconds.

Using Connect Scenes in Small Groups (15 minutes a day for a week)

1. By now, students should be enjoying the activity and getting better at coming up with ideas for connecting scenes. Combine pairs so that you have groups of four.

2. Have each member of the group choose a number between one and four. Call out, "Number 2 and Number 4" and ask them to get up and be prepared to start the connect scene that was introduced on page 174. Give them the signal and say "freeze!" after 10 to 15 seconds.

3. Now call out "Number 3." The student who is number three has to look at both frozen students and decide what new scene could be made. Number 3 then "taps out" one of the students on the shoulder (i.e., Number 2). That is the signal for that student to leave the scene and sit down. Number 3 then assumes the exact same

body position as the student who was "tapped out" and when the teacher says "connect," Number 3 starts a new scene. The Connect Scenes continue as before, except that the teacher designates a new number to enter the scene with each change.

4. Once the teacher feels that students understand what to do, the members of each group can be tasked with saying "freeze" and "connect" to rotate students into the scenes over the course of 2 minutes or so. The students can proceed in number order or randomly, as long as everyone gets in over the allotted time.

5. The most important difference in the activity now is that, instead of a definite 10 to 15 seconds between scenes, they go on until a student sees the scene members in body positions that they think they can connect to and then says, "freeze!" Once he/she has tapped out a student, that student can say "connect!" to start the new scene.

KEEN Considerations When Using CONNECT SCENES in Groups

- Groups can sometimes have problems by letting the scenes go too long before freezing them. To remedy this, set a time of either 2 or 3 minutes and require that everyone be in at least one scene by that time. They will get better at it!

- This is a good time to have a debrief after each group session, asking students to volunteer suggestions to make the *Connect Scenes* proceed more smoothly. You may be surprised at how many previously unengaged students contribute to this discussion!

Using Connect Scenes with the Curriculum

Once students are familiar with Connect Scenes there are innumerable way that the strategy can be applied across the curriculum to help students understand, process, and demonstrate their ability to manipulate curriculum material. Below are some examples for each age group!

Grades K-3

1. *Ways to Making Friends* – Have each scene show a different way to make friends and be a good one.

2. *Seasons* – Show the effects of each season on the earth, people, and/or animals.

   Reading Comprehension – Each different scene can be required to make a different connection in one of the following areas:
   - text to text
   - text to self
   - text to world

3. *Science and Technology: Simple Machines* – Create connecting scenes that demonstrate the differences between various simple machines and how they work.

4. *Math: Sorting and Grouping* – Each scene demonstrates a different way to group common objects (i.e., cars) based on their attributes.

Hints for this Age Group

- Many of these will need to be practiced by the students before they are presented to the teacher. This may take time, but it is highly effective time. Allow students the time they need, knowing that four students debating how to demonstrate an example of a simple machine and then physically demonstrating it in *Connect Scene* is a much higher level of engagement, cognition, and ownership of the curriculum than would exist if those students were simply listening to a presentation from the teacher.

- Discussion after *Connect Scenes* is a critical component for developing oral language skills among struggling students. Ask them to explain and justify their choices (i.e., "Why did you choose that part for the beginning of your story in your first *Connect Scene*? Why was it important?")

- You can share examples of effective connections from one scene to the next where the body positioning the group chose was seamless and evoked a "wow...cool!" reaction from you.

- Because of differences in how boys and girls learn, single-sex groupings can be useful here.

Grades 4-6

1. *Language: Fostering Expanded Vocabulary And Word Choice* – Give groups a word (e.g., walking) and challenge them to come up with as many 15-second Connect Scenes as they can that demonstrate synonyms or variations on the meaning of that word (strolling, ambling, limping, etc.)

2. *Writing: Story Starters* – Giving them a 5-minute time limit, challenge groups to create as many connect scenes as possible that show how a mystery could start.

3. *Environmental Studies* – Each Connect Scene demonstrates a positive action for the environment that can be taken at home by a 10-year-old

4. *Medieval Times: Daily Life* – Each Connect Scene must show a day in the life of
    *   Peasant/Serf
    *   Guild Member
    *   Noble
    *   King

5. *Math: Patterning* – Successive scenes demonstrating different patterns in math

Hints for this Age Group

*   As with the earlier age group, practice time is important here

- If there are a significant number of details to be included in the Connect Scenes (e.g. the medieval times scenes must highlight the food, clothing, work, and leisure time of each group), students can be asked to create outlines that the teacher can see before or after the group prepares the scenes.

- *Connect Scenes* can be an excellent form of non-paper/pencil authentic assessment, particularly when debrief questioning and discussion allows the teacher to probe for student understanding.

- Having heterogeneous groupings allow for this strategy to be effective for community-building in the class as well as reducing the cognitive diversity among students relating to the curriculum being studied

Grades 7-10

1. *Chemistry: Elements and Compounds* – Each scene describes a different one, giving the properties that determine its practical uses.

2. *English: Themes in a Novel* – Connect Scenes must demonstrate various examples of hubris found in Macbeth and link them to similar modern examples.

3. *History: The Conscription Crisis of 1917* – Representations of the how different groups in society felt about conscription and why.

4. *Geometry: Pythagorean Theorem* – Scenes demonstrate the theorem and its practical applications.

5. *Civics* – Scenes examine the concept of "power" as it is influenced by gender, race, social position, and wealth.

Hints for this Age Group

- Connect Scenes are great remedies for the scourge of boring classroom presentations that are often found in middle and high school classrooms. Even though the teacher's assessment is being done related to the content being presented, the nature of Connect Scenes causes the participants to pay more attention to the aesthetics surrounding curriculum content and they can be quite enjoyable and even compelling to watch.

- Discussing ways to be creative in the transitions between scenes (i.e., using a *slo-mo* approach) can generate great enthusiasm for creating *Connect Scenes* that are both engaging and satisfying learning experience for everyone involved. They easily foster "meaningful work" and its attendant passion and enthusiasm.

- *Connect Scenes* can easily be part of a multifaceted learning/assessment process that might involve any of the following:
  - *Note-taking from text*
  - *Creation of an outline*
  - *A written essay*
  - *Artwork and visual representations*
  - *A video presentation*

Variations And Extensions That Deepen Learning

If *Connect Scenes* are working well for you and your students, you may want to consider periodic whole-group sessions. They must be done in a spirit of playfulness that assures voluntary participation with no student required to be in any scene, but they can be a fun way to spur creative thinking while reviewing curriculum material.

Large Group Connect Scenes

1. Space is cleared and everyone sits in a circle.
2. The teacher specifies the theme for Connect Scenes (i.e., "Each new scene must represent at least one new fact we have learned about the history and makeup of the earth's crust."
3. Two students come up and the teacher asks them to start a connect scene meeting the criteria.
4. Any other student can call "freeze!" and then take the place of one of the students and continue a new scene.
5. The goal is to see how many can be created in 2 minutes.
6. Students should be encouraged to make the storylines funny and outlandish even as the content is correct.

Add-On Connect Scenes

1. Start Connect Scenes

2. When a student freezes a scene, does not tap out anyone, but steps into the scene and assumes a body position, that will allow them to start the new scene they have in mind. The other two students go along with the scene once it is started.

3. See how many students and new scenes can be added in a 3- to 5-minute timeframe—all the while staying within the theme and criteria specified by the teacher!

CHAPTER 15
KEEN Conclusions

"This has been the most profound professional development experience that I've had in 11 years of teaching."
—Elementary school teacher at the end of KEEN training

Making It Happen

We now come to the part of the book that relies more on you than me. If I have done my job well, you have a good understanding of the challenges that struggling learners face, why they need a different approach in the classroom, and why both the brain research and anecdotal experiences of teachers support the use of KEEN strategies as part of classroom instruction. More importantly, you should be keen to see this approach taken in the classrooms where you are connected.

If you are a teacher, you will hopefully try at least one KEEN strategy the next time you are with your students. If you are a principal, you have something to share with your teachers that can make a difference not just in the classrooms in your school, but also in the number of children who show up at the office because they are not doing their work or disrupting class. Let's face it: Kids passionately engaged in learning in the classroom rarely show up to the office except for good reasons, like to show off evidence of their success. If you are a parent who despairs because your child—who for the first 5 years of life couldn't learn enough and was busily into everything—does not succeed in school now and rarely seems to demonstrate the potential you know is there, then you can give this book to your child's teacher, principal, or school parent council, explaining to them that it has some helpful ideas about differentiated instruction that you believe would help your child and others in the school.

Beyond classroom use, nothing prevents parents from doing the activities with their children at home. If your child has to write a story for creative writing, for example, why not let them create Still Life images (see page 110) of the major events in the story? Do it with them yourself—you'll be surprised how much fun you'll have!—or draft siblings and friends to freeze as needed. For that matter, get the neighbours' kids involved and let everyone help each other with a KEEN approach to the evening's homework. Whatever you do, don't give up. Your child was born to learn. As parents, we know that in our gut, and that is why it is so distressing to see that kid we know has so much to give, selling himself or herself short because of their lack of success in class. But together we can change that.

Finally, if you are an "educational influencer," someone who is a researcher, writer, consultant, ministry of education, or district superintendent or director, this book will hopefully spur you to investigate further how strategies like this can become part of the teaching practice in the educational institutions you care about. There are many different educational fads that those of us who work in education need to be wary of, but the approach outlined here is one that is easily validated and simple enough to implement, in part because it's so enjoyable for teachers and their students.

Keen Professional Development for Teachers

The strategies that have been shared in this book were refined through a process that involved thousands of students and their teachers, who were able to apply them to their own students and curricula. During that process, we discovered that the most effective way to make sure the strategies were understood and implemented, so that they became a regular part of the classroom activities, was to coach teachers in their use over a number of weeks. This idea of embedded professional development has been increasingly acknowledged over the past few years the most effective way to help teachers improve their practice.

We know that the single-day offsite "PD workshops" for teachers have a very poor record of affecting classroom practice afterward. There are many reasons for this. The reality of a workshop space is often very different from that of the classroom space. Teachers are busy individuals with many responsibilities, and their focus is primarily on daily classroom tasks; if there is not a direct connection to those tasks in their professional development, teaching practice will not change. Most importantly, when teachers run into problems when trying new strategies (known as the "implementation dip"), there is often nowhere to turn for support and it is easier for us as teachers to just let the new approach fade into the background with the idea that we'll get to it later. But of course we rarely do. In the end, ineffective professional development is a large waste of time and money.

Our approach is different. We introduce each strategy weekly over a number of weeks. Our coaches are there to make sure it applies to the teacher's curriculum so it is not considered an "add-on" but rather a fun, easy way to reach the curriculum goals they have for their students. Teachers can ask questions and share challenges as they apply KEEN learning and this, in turn, increases commitment to the strategies and helps the teachers develop competency with them in an amazingly short period of time.

It is true that this method takes longer and costs a bit more than a 1-day workshop, but the educational benefits for students of not removing a teacher from their classroom for training, combined with savings generated by needing fewer supply teacher days for teacher development, should also be considered. More importantly, the investments in educational leverage for a teacher who deeply understands and commits to this approach are huge; it can change a teacher's practice henceforth. Think about that for a moment: How many thousands of students will a 25-year-old teacher affect over a career? How many colleagues will that teacher influence? In the end, fostering embedded professional development for teachers is the one of the most cost-effective things we can do in education.

The KEEN Differentiated Learning Group is a nonprofit organization dedicated to providing this type of experience to teachers. If you would like more information, please visit www.keenforlearning.org.

What About Those Students Who Don't Struggle?

This may seem like a strange place to leave off our discussion in this book, but it's important to recognize that the majority of students do indeed succeed in our school system and one might fear that an approach dedicated to the struggling learner might shortchange them. That is not the case. One of the great ironies is that the differentiated approach reflected in this book is often more in demand in classrooms known to be populated with "enriched" or higher achievers.

One of the most enlightening/frustrating conversations I ever had about this was with a consultant of a local school district who said, "Ed, in Enrichment, we do this kind of stuff all the time…" He knew that activities like this unleashed tremendous creativity and developed higher-order thinking skills in students. Additionally, the parents of these students demanded that they be offered such learning opportunities. That made me more determined than ever to see these strategies introduced in a way that would help struggling students who, like Chad, were much more at risk in our education system. And that is why I made struggling students the focus of this book. However—now that the cat's out of the bag—I will happily admit that they are indeed incredibly useful for higher-achieving students, many of whom are just as bored with traditional classroom activities but, because they have one of the motivations discussed in Chapter 2, they put in their time and do what's expected. But they cannot reach their full potential in the classroom like that!

Using KEEN activities for these students entices them into "upping their game" with more effort and achievement because they enjoy the creative possibilities they discover as they participate. We saw this firsthand at the beginning of our work: French Immersion and Enriched schools were the earliest institutions to invite us into their classrooms. They wanted to push their students to the highest levels of achievement and thinking and saw that possibility in this approach. Now schools of all types have come to believe in its benefits.

Perhaps the best way to understand this is to see that it reflects the old educational saw that "Good teaching is good teaching." KEEN differentiated learning is simply good teaching. And the best part of all is that KEEN activities can be used *at the same time with both enriched and struggling students, providing equal opportunities for all learners, who can take what they need from the activity and benefit at an individual level appropriate to their ability.* That sounds like a pretty good definition of differentiated instruction, come to think of it. May your explorations into the new world of KEEN learning be helpful in reaching struggling kids, like my friend Chad, and persuading them not to give up on themselves in the classroom—or in life.

NOTES

Chapter 1 - Classroom Learning and Life

p. 9 "They even live longer!"

Baum, S., & Ma, J. (2007). Education pays: The benefits of higher education for individuals and society. College Board. Retrieved April 12, 2010, from http://www.collegeboard.com/prod_downloads/about/news_info/cbsenior/yr2007/ed-pays-2007.pdf

Bureau of Labor Statistics. (2009). Employment projects: Education pays. U.S. Department of Labor. Retrieved June 23, 2010, from http://www.bls.gov/emp/ep_chart_001.htm

Ungerleider, Ch. (2004). The social determinants of health: Education as a determinant of health. Public Health Agency of Canada. Retrieved July 3, 2010, from http://www.phac-aspc.gc.ca/ph-sp/oi-ar/10_education-eng.php

"and quality of life indicators" UNESCO. "Education for All" Web site. Retrieved June 23, 2010, from http://www.unesco.org/en/efa/

"increasing spending on education by" For statistics by country see:

United States: U.S. Department of Education. (2004). Annual secondary education expenditures per student. Retrieved June 15, 2010, from http://www2.ed.gov/about/overview/fed/10facts/edlite-chart.html

Canada: Brockington, R. (2009). Summary public school indicators for the provinces and territories, 2000/2001 to 2006/2007. Statistics Canada. Retrieved February 3, 2010, from http://www.statcan.gc.ca/pub/81-595-m/81-595-m2009078-eng.pdf

World: UNESCO. (2007). Global Education Digest 2007. Retrieved June 13, 2010, from http://www.uis.unesco.org/ev.php?ID=7167_201&ID2=DO_TOPIC

p. 10 "depending on how it is tabulated" Heckman, J. J, & LaFontaine, P. A. (2007). The American high school graduation rate: Trends and levels. NBER Working Paper No. 13670. Retrieved May 30, 2010, from http://buildingbrightfutures.net/Post/sections/42/Files/The%20American%20High%20School%20Graduation%20Rate.pdf

p.11 "learning for the rest of their lives" A number of authors discuss this phenomenon:

Dweck, C., & Elliott, E. (1988). Goals: An approach to motivation and achievement. Journal of Personality and Social Psychology, 54(1), 5-12.

Seligman, Martin. 1990. Learned Optimism. New York, NY: Pocket Books.

Schunk, D. H. (1984). Self-efficacy perspective on achievement behavior. Educational Psychologist, 19(1), 48-58.

p. 12 "how the world "actually" works." Murphy, J. T. S., n.d. Failure in school as nothing to do with success in life! Ezine Articles. Retrieved June 3, 2010, from http://ezinearticles.com/?Failure-in-School-Has-Nothing-to-Do-With-Success-in-Life!&id=4062893

Chapter 2 - A Littered Landscape

p. 18 *"catalysts for their achievements"* Doskoch, P. (2005). The winning edge. Psychology Today. Retrieved May 14, 2010, from http://www.psychologytoday.com/articles/200510/the-winning-edge?page=2

p. 19 *"makes many people unhappy and dissatisfied"* For Canada: Canadian Education Association. (2007). Public attitudes towards education in Canada: The 2007 CEA Survey. Retrieved June 23, 2010, from http://www.cea-ace.ca/res.cfm?subsection=rep&page=publiced&subpage=ch2

United States: CBC News. (2009). Most U.S. parents like their kids' schools: poll. Retrieved April 6, 2010, from http://www.cbc.ca/consumer/story/2009/08/24/us-school-satisfaction-poll.html#ixzz0uzOuyrDF

"grade inflation, or student cheating" Gulli, C., Kohler, N., & Patriquin, M. (2007). The great university cheating scandal. Macleans.ca. Retrieved June 15, 2010, from http://www.macleans.ca/homepage/magazine/article.jsp?content=20070209_174847_6984

p. 21 *"particularly large for minority students"* Greene, J. P., & Winters, M. A. (2006) Leaving boys behind: Public high school graduation rates. Manhattan Institute Civic Report 48 (pp. 69-88). Retrieved June 18, 2010, from http://www.manhattan-institute.org/html/cr_48.htm

"much higher rate for minority students" Statistics Canada. (2005). Thousands of drop-outs and drop-out rate, Canada and provinces (table). Retrieved June 3, 2010, from http://www.statcan.gc.ca/pub/81-004-x/2005004/8984-eng.htm#table2

"averaged nearly 40%!" Brown, R. S. (2010). The TDSB grade 9 cohort study of Fall 2004. Toronto, Ontario, Canada: Toronto District School Board. Retrieved June 23, 2010, from http://www.tdsb.on.ca/wwwdocuments/about_us/external_research_application/docs/TheGrade9CohortOfFall2004.pdf

"and 74% in Canada" National Dropout Prevention Center, n.d. Top 5 reasons to stay in school. Retrieved June 23, 2010, from http://www.dropoutprevention.org/resource/family_student/reasons.htm

p. 26 Frankl, V. E. (1963). Man's search for meaning: An introduction to logotherapy (Rev. ed.). New York, NY: Washington Square Press.

Maslow, A. (1954). Motivation and personality. New York, NY: Harper and Row.

Chapter 3 - Meaningful Learning in a Connected World

p. 30 *"Did You know"* Fisch, K. (2007). Did You Know 2.0. YouTube. Retrieved July 3, 2010, from http://www.youtube.com/watch?v=pMcfrLYDm2U&feature=related

p. 31 *"at least $680 billion"* Quelch, J. (2009). Quantifying the economic impact of the Internet. Harvard Business School, Faculty Research. Retrieved June 24, 2010, from http://hbswk.hbs.edu/item/6268.html

p. 32 *"business-networking site Ecademy"* Powers, P. (2009). What jobs will exist in 10-20 years? Ecademy. Retrieved June 24, 2010, from http://www.ecademy.com/node.php?id=133367

"Authors such as Thomas Freidman" Friedman, T. L. (2006). The world is flat: A brief history of the twenty-first century (Rev. ed.). New York, NY: Farrar.

p. 33 *"the Conference Board of Canada"* OECD. (2009). Education at a glance. The Conference Board of Canada. Retrieved June 3, 2010, from http://www.conferenceboard.ca/hcp/details/education.aspx#link

p. 38 *"on which students are tested in Ontario"* Ontario Ministry of Education and Training. (2004). Literacy for learning: The report of the expert panel on literacy in grades 4 to 6 in Ontario. Toronto, Ontario, Canada: Ontario Ministry of Education and Training.

p. 39 *"The Story of Success"* Gladwell, M. (2008). Outliers: The story of success (1st ed.). New York, NY: Little, Brown and Company.

Chapter 4 - Getting Our Heads Around the Brain Science

p. 43 The quote that starts this chapter is from an OECD conference of the brain and learning: OECD. (2002). *Understanding the brain: Towards a new learning science.* Danvers, MA: Organization for Economic Cooperation and Development. Retrieved June 23, 2010, from http://link.library.utoronto.ca.myaccess.library.utoronto.ca/eir/EIRdetail.cfm?Resources__ID=217161&T=F

p. 46 *"strengthening or weakening of existing ones"* See the following resources:

Blakemore, S. (2005). In U. Frith (Ed.), *The learning brain: Lessons for education*. Alexandria, VA: Association for Supervision and Curriculum Development.

Sylwester, R. (1995). *A celebration of neurons: An educator's guide to the human brain*. Alexandria, VA: Association for Supervision and Curriculum Development.

"even after injury or in old age." Doidge, N. (2007). *The brain that changes itself: Stories of personal triumph from the frontiers of brain science*. New York, NY: Viking.

"traced to communication between neurons." Wolfe, P. (2001). *Brain matters: Translating research into classroom practice*. Alexandra, VA: Association for Supervision and Curriculum Development.

p. 48 *"Neuroscientist Michael Gazzaniga"* Gazzaniga, M. S. (1998). The mind's past. Berkeley, CA: University of California Press.

Chapter 5 - Fear and Loathing in the Classroom

p. 53 *"The amygdala, one of the most primitive parts"* LeDoux, J. E. (1996). The emotional brain: *The mysterious underpinnings of emotional life*. Toronto, Ontario, Canada: Simon & Schuster.

p. 56 *"not to mention bodily health."* Wolfe, P. (2001). *Brain matters: Translating research into classroom practice*. Alexandra, VA: Association for Supervision and Curriculum Development.

p. 57 *"Howard Gardner and others"* Silver, H. F. (2000). In R. W. Strong & M. J. Perini (Eds.), So each may learn: *Integrating learning styles and multiple intelligences*. Alexandria, VA: Association for Supervision and Curriculum Development.

p. 61 *"Dr Leonard Sax"* Sax, L. (2005). *Why gender matters: What parents and teachers need to know about the emerging science of sex differences* (1st ed.). New York, NY: Doubleday.

p. 63 *" Lorraine Brizendine"* Brizendine, L. (2006). *The female brain.* New York, NY: Morgan Road Books.

p. 67 Quote from Sax, L. (2007). *Boys adrift: Five factors driving the growing epidemic of unmotivated boys and underachieving young men.* New York, NY: Basic Books.

p. 68 *"Martin Seligman terms Learned Helplessness"* Peterson, C. (1993). In S. F. Maier & M. E. P. Seligman (Eds.), *Learned helplessness: A theory for the age of personal control.* New York, NY: Oxford University Press.

Chapter 7 - The Elements of KEEN Differentiated Learning

p. 83 *"for learning and self-expression"* Gardner, H. (2004). *Frames of mind: The theory of multiple intelligences* (20th anniversary ed.). New York, NY: Basic Books.

"Eric Jensen, in his book" Jensen, E. (2001). *Arts with the brain in mind.* Alexandria, VA: Association for Supervision and Curriculum Development.

p. 84 *"kinesthetic is the reason for this success"* Jensen, E. (2006). *Enriching the brain: How to maximize every learner's potential* (1st ed.). San Francisco, CA: Jossey-Bass.

"that may influence memory and learning" Bower, J. M., & Parsons, L. M. (2003). Rethinking the "lesser brain." *Scientific American, 289*(2), 51.

"usually occur in the frontal lobe" Jossey-Bass Inc. (2008). *The Jossey-Bass reader on the brain and learning* (1st ed.). San Francisco, CA: Jossey-Bass.

p. 86 *"the most basic of biological needs"* Brown, S. L. (2009). In C. C. Vaughan (Ed.), Play: *How it shapes the brain, opens the imagination, and invigorates the soul.* New York, NY: Avery.

p. 87 *"Researchers Kerr and Apter"* Kerr, J. H., & Apter, M. J. (1991). *Adult play: A reversal theory approach* (pp. 167-174). Berwyn, PA: Swets & Zeitlinger.

"associated with reducing stress levels" Bennett, M. P., Zeller, J. M., Rosenberg, L., & McCann, J. (2003). The effect of mirthful laughter on stress and natural killer cell activity. *Alternative Therapies in Health and Medicine*, 9(2), 38-43.

p. 88 *"general overall health improvement"* Fry Jr., W. F. (1992). The physiologic effects of humor, mirth, and laughter. *JAMA, 267*, 1857-1858.

"that occurs when we laugh" Sousa, D. A. (2001). *How the brain learns: A classroom teacher's guide.* Thousand Oaks, CA: Corwin Press.

"Blatner and Blatner" Blatner, A. (1997). Blatner, A. (1997). In A. Blatner (Ed.), *The art of play: Helping adults reclaim imagination and spontaneity* (Rev. ed.). New York, NY: Brunner/Mazel.

p. 88 *"increased focus and attention span"* Sousa, D. A. (2001). *How the brain learns: A classroom teacher's guide.* Thousand Oaks, CA: Corwin Press.

p. 89 *"mind and work themselves out."* Brown, S. L. (2009). In C. C. Vaughan (Ed.), *Play: How it shapes the brain, opens the imagination, and invigorates the soul.* New York, NY: Avery.

p. 91 *"the space we call reality"* Covey, S. R. (1990). *The seven habits of highly effective people: Restoring the character ethic* (1st ed.). London, England: Fireside.

"direct impact on learning and cognitive function" Jossey-Bass Inc. (2008). *The Jossey-Bass reader on the brain and learning* (1st ed.). San Francisco, CA: Jossey-Bass.

"link between cognitive function and emotion" Kober, H., Barrett, L. F., Joseph, J., Bliss-Moreau, E., Lindquist, K., & Wager, T. D. (2008). Functional grouping and cortical-

subcortical interactions in emotion: A meta-analysis of neuroimaging studies. *NeuroImage*, 42(2), 998-1031.

p. 91 *"Remembrance of Emotions Past"* Jossey-Bass Inc. (2008). Jossey-Bass Inc. (2008). *The Jossey-Bass reader on the brain and learning* (1st ed.). San Francisco, CA: Jossey-Bass.

p. 92 *"bizarre events stay in our memory"* Davidson, D. (2006). *Memory for bizarre and other unusual events: Evidence from script research* (pp. 157-179). New York, NY: Oxford University Press.

"seem to help jog memory function" Satow, T., Usui, K., Matsuhashi, M., Yamamoto, J., Begum, T., Shibasaki, H., et al. (2003). Mirth and laughter arising from human temporal cortex. *Journal of Neurology, Neurosurgery, and Psychiatry*, 74(7), 1004-1005.

p. 93 *what Elliot Eisner calls "representation"* Jossey-Bass Inc. (2008). *The Jossey-Bass reader on the brain and learning* (1st ed.). San Francisco, CA: Jossey-Bass.

"and stimuli that we experience daily" Modell, A. H. (2003). *Imagination and the meaningful brain*. Cambridge, MA: MIT Press.

p.94 *"where they originally learned the material"* Gregory, G. (2007). In C. Chapman (Ed.), *Differentiated instructional strategies: One size doesn't fit all* (2nd ed.). Thousand Oaks, CA: Corwin Press.

p. 94 *"Famed psychologist Jerome Bruner"* Bruner, J. S. (1983). *In search of mind: Essays in autobiography* (1st ed.). New York, NY: Harper & Row.

p. 95 *"the more fully developed we are"* Brockmeier, J., & Carbaugh, D. A. (Eds.). (2001). *Narrative and identity: Studies in autobiography, self, and culture*. Philadelphia, PA: John Benjamins Publishing.

"allowed to create stories using drama David Booth" For more information see:

Booth, D. (1985). "Imaginary gardens with real toads": Reading and drama in education. *Theory into Practice, 24*(3), 193-198.

Booth, D. (2005). *Story drama: Creating stories through role playing, improvising, and reading aloud* (2nd ed.). Markham, Ontario, Canada: Pembroke Publishers.

"unity to our understanding of life" Neisser, U., & Fivush, R. (Eds.). (1994). *The remembering self: Construction and accuracy in the self-narrative.* New York, NY: Cambridge University Press.

"of how the world works" Brown, S. L. (2009). In C. C. Vaughan (Ed.), *Play: How it shapes the brain, opens the imagination, and invigorates the soul.* New York, NY: Avery.

p. 97 *"zone of proximal development"* Vygotski, L. S. (1978). In M. Cole (Ed.), *Mind in society: The development of higher psychological processes.* Cambridge, MA: Harvard University Press.

p. 100 *"a previous book upon it"* Dixon, E. J. (2006). *Literacy through drama.* Barrie, Ontario, Canada: Wintertickle Press.

Chapter 15 - KEEN Conclusions

p. 194 *"helping teachers improve their practice afterward"* See:

Haqq, Abdal (1996). Making time for teacher professional development. *ERIC Digest.* Washington, DC: ERIC Clearinghouse on Teaching and Teacher Education.

Adey, P. (2004). *The professional development of teachers: Practice and theory.* Boston, MA: Kluwer Academic.

"implementation dip" Fullan, M. (2006). In C. St. Germain & Ontario Principals Council (Eds.), *Learning places: A field guide for improving the context of schooling.* Thousand Oaks, CA: Corwin Press.

p. 194-95 For a good summary of the types of professional
    development available to teachers and the value of various
    models see: The Literacy and Numeracy Secretariat's
    Coaching Institute for Literacy and Numeracy Leaders.
    (2004). Improving Student Achievement In Literacy And
    Numeracy: Job-Embedded Professional Learning. June
    3, 2010, from http://www.eworkshop.on.ca/edu/pdf/
    Mod42_prof_learn.pdf

Bibliography

Adey, P. (2004). *The professional development of teachers: Practice and theory.* Boston, MA: Kluwer Academic.

Baum, S., & Ma, J. (2007). Education pays: The benefits of higher education for individuals and society. College Board. Retrieved April 12, 2010, from http://www.collegeboard.com/prod_downloads/about/news_info/cbsenior/yr2007/ed-pays-2007.pdf

Bennett, M. P., Zeller, J. M., Rosenberg, L., & McCann, J. (2003). The effect of mirthful laughter on stress and natural killer cell activity. *Alternative Therapies in Health and Medicine, 9*(2), 38-43.

Blakemore, S. (2005). In U. Frith (Ed.), *The learning brain: Lessons for education.* Alexandria, VA: Association for Supervision and Curriculum Development.

Blatner, A. (1997). In A. Blatner (Ed.), *The art of play: Helping adults reclaim imagination and spontaneity* (Rev. ed.). New York, NY: Brunner/Mazel.

Booth, D. (1985). "Imaginary gardens with real toads": Reading and drama in education. *Theory into Practice, 24*(3), 193-198.

Booth, D. (2005). *Story drama: Creating stories through role playing, improvising, and reading aloud* (2nd ed.). Markham, Ontario, Canada: Pembroke Publishers.

Bower, J. M., & Parsons, L. M. (2003). Rethinking the "lesser brain." *Scientific American, 289*(2), 51.

Brizendine, L. (2006). *The female brain.* New York, NY: Morgan Road Books.

Brockington, R. (2009). Summary public school indicators for the provinces and territories, 2000/2001 to 2006/2007. Statistics Canada. Retrieved February 3, 2010, from http://www.statcan.gc.ca/pub/81-595-m/81-595-m2009078-eng.pdf

Brockmeier, J., & Carbaugh, D. A. (Eds.). (2001). *Narrative and identity: Studies in autobiography, self, and culture.* Philadelphia, PA: John Benjamins Publishing.

Brown, R. S. (2010). *The TDSB grade 9 cohort study of Fall 2004.* Toronto, Ontario, Canada: Toronto District School Board. Retrieved June 23, 2010, from http://www.tdsb.on.ca/ wwwdocuments/about_us/external_research_application/ docs/TheGrade9CohortOfFall2004.pdf

Brown, S. L. (2009). In C. C. Vaughan (Ed.), *Play: How it shapes the brain, opens the imagination, and invigorates the soul.* New York, NY: Avery.

Bruner, J. S. (1983). *In search of mind: Essays in autobiography* (1st ed.). New York, NY: Harper & Row.

Bureau of Labor Statistics. (2009). Employment projects: Education pays. U.S. Department of Labor. Retrieved June 23, 2010, from http://www.bls.gov/emp/ep_chart_001.htm

Canadian Education Association. (2007). Public attitudes towards education in Canada: The 2007 CEA Survey. Retrieved June 23, 2010, from http://www.cea-ace.ca/res.cf m?subsection=rep&page=publiced&subpage=ch2

CBC News. (2009). Most U.S. parents like their kids' schools: poll. Retrieved April 6, 2010, from http://www.cbc.ca/ consumer/story/2009/08/24/us-school-satisfaction-poll. html#ixzz0uzOuyrDF"

The Conference Board of Canada (2010). Employability skills 2000+. Retrieved June 24, 2010, from http://www. conferenceboard.ca/topics/education/learning-tools/ employability-skills.aspx

Covey, S. R. (1990). *The seven habits of highly effective people: Restoring the character ethic* (1st ed.). London, England: Fireside.

Davidson, D. (2006). *Memory for bizarre and other unusual events: Evidence from script research* (pp. 157-179). New York, NY: Oxford University Press.

Dixon, E. J. (2006). *Literacy through drama.* Barrie, Ontario, Canada: Wintertickle Press.

Doidge, N. (2007). *The brain that changes itself: Stories of personal triumph from the frontiers of brain science.* New York, NY: Viking.

Doskoch, P. (2005). The winning edge. *Psychology Today.* Retrieved May 14, 2010 from http://www.psychologytoday. com/articles/200510/the-winning-edge?page=2

Dweck, C., & Elliott, E. (1988). Goals: An approach to motivation and achievement. *Journal of Personality and Social Psychology, 54*(1), 5-12.

Fisch, K. (2007). Did You Know 2.0. YouTube. Retrieved July 3, 2010, from http://www.youtube.com/watch?v=pMcfrLY Dm2U&feature=related

Frankl, V. E. (1963). *Man's search for meaning: An introduction to logotherapy* (Rev. ed.). New York, NY: Washington Square Press.

Friedman, T. L. (2006). *The world is flat: A brief history of the twenty-first century* (Rev. ed.). New York, NY: Farrar.

Fry Jr., W. F. (1992). The physiologic effects of humor, mirth, and laughter. *JAMA, 267*, 1857-1858.

Fullan, M. (2006). In C. St. Germain & Ontario Principals Council (Eds.), Learning places: *A field guide for improving the context of schooling.* Thousand Oaks, CA: Corwin Press.

Gardner, H. (2004). *Frames of mind: The theory of multiple intelligences* (20th anniversary ed.). New York, NY: Basic Books.

Gazzaniga, M. S. (1998). *The mind's past.* Berkeley, CA: University of California Press.

Gladwell, M. (2008). *Outliers: The story of success* (1st ed.). New York, NY: Little, Brown and Company.

Greene, J. P., & Winters, M. A. (2006) *Leaving boys behind: Public high school graduation rates.* Manhattan Institute Civic Report 48 (pp. 69-88). Retrieved June 18, 2010, from http://www.manhattan-institute.org/html/cr_48.htm

Gregory, G. (2007). In C. Chapman (Ed.), *Differentiated instructional strategies: One size doesn't fit all* (2nd ed.). Thousand Oaks, CA: Corwin Press.

Gulli, C., Kohler, N., & Patriquin, M. (2007). The great university cheating scandal. Macleans.ca. Retrieved June 15, 2010, from http://www.macleans.ca/homepage/ magazine/article.jsp?content=20070209_174847_6984

Haqq, Abdal (1996). Making time for teacher professional development. *ERIC Digest.* Washington, DC: ERIC Clearinghouse on Teaching and Teacher Education.

The Literacy and Numeracy Secretariat's Coaching Institute for Literacy and Numeracy Leaders. (2004). Improving Student Achievement In Literacy And Numeracy: Job-Embedded Professional Learning. Retrieved June 3, 2010, from http://www.eworkshop.on.ca/edu/pdf/Mod42_prof_learn.pdf

Heckman, J. J, & LaFontaine, P. A. (2007). The American high school graduation rate: Trends and levels. NBER Working Paper No. 13670. May 30, 2010, from http://buildingbrightfutures.net/Post/sections/42/Files/The%20American%20High%20School%20Graduation%20Rate.pdf

Jensen, E. (2001). *Arts with the brain in mind.* Alexandria, VA: Association for Supervision and Curriculum Development.

Jensen, E. (2006). *Enriching the brain: How to maximize every learner's potentia*l (1st ed.). San Francisco, CA: Jossey-Bass.

Jossey-Bass Inc. (2008). *The Jossey-Bass reader on the brain and learning* (1st ed.). San Francisco, CA: Jossey-Bass.

Kerr, J. H., & Apter, M. J. (1991). *Adult play: A reversal theory approach* (pp. 167-174). Berwyn, PA: Swets & Zeitlinger.

Kober, H., Barrett, L. F., Joseph, J., Bliss-Moreau, E., Lindquist, K., & Wager, T. D. (2008). Functional grouping and cortical-subcortical interactions in emotion: A meta-analysis of neuroimaging studies. *NeuroImage, 42*(2), 998-1031.

LeDoux, J. E. (1996). *The emotional brain: The mysterious underpinnings of emotional life.* Toronto, Ontario, Canada: Simon & Schuster.

Maslow, A. (1954). *Motivation and personality.* New York, NY: Harper and Row.

Modell, A. H. (2003). *Imagination and the meaningful brain.* Cambridge, MA: MIT Press.

Murphy, J. T. S., n.d. Failure in school as nothing to do with success in life! Ezine Articles. Retrieved June 3, 2010, from http://ezinearticles.com/?Failure-in-School-Has-Nothing-to-Do-With-Success-in-Life!&id=4062893

National Dropout Prevention Center, n.d. Top 5 reasons to stay in school. Retrieved Month XX, 2010, from http://www.dropoutprevention.org/resource/family_student/reasons.htm

Neisser, U., & Fivush, R. (Eds.). (1994). *The remembering self: Construction and accuracy in the self-narrative.* New York, NY: Cambridge University Press.

OECD. (2009). *Education at a glance.* The Conference Board of Canada. Retrieved June 3, 2010, from http://www.conferenceboard.ca/hcp/details/education.aspx#link

Ontario Ministry of Education and Training. (2004). *Literacy for learning: The report of the expert panel on literacy in grades 4 to 6 in Ontario.* Toronto, Ontario, Canada: Ontario Ministry of Education and Training.

Peterson, C. (1993). In S. F. Maier & M. E. P. Seligman (Eds.), *Learned helplessness: A theory for the age of personal control.* New York, NY: Oxford University Press.

Powers, P. (2009). What jobs will exist in 10-20 years? Ecademy. Retrieved June 24, 2010, from http://www.ecademy.com/node.php?id=133367

Quelch, J. (2009). Quantifying the economic impact of the Internet. Harvard Business School, Faculty Research. Retrieved June 24, 2010, from http://hbswk.hbs.edu/item/6268.html

Satow, T., Usui, K., Matsuhashi, M., Yamamoto, J., Begum, T., Shibasaki, H., et al. (2003). Mirth and laughter arising from human temporal cortex. Journal of Neurology, *Neurosurgery, and Psychiatry, 74*(7), 1004-1005.

Sax, L. (2005). *Why gender matters: What parents and teachers need to know about the emerging science of sex differences* (1st ed.). New York, NY: Doubleday.

Sax, L. (2007). *Boys adrift: Five factors driving the growing epidemic of unmotivated boys and underachieving young men.* New York, NY: Basic Books.

Schunk, D. H. (1984). Self-efficacy perspective on achievement behavior. *Educational Psychologist, 19*(1), 48-58.

Seligman, Martin. 1990. *Learned Optimism.* New York, NY: Pocket Books.

Silver, H. F. (2000). In R. W. Strong & M. J. Perini (Eds.), *So each may learn: Integrating learning styles and multiple intelligences.* Alexandria, VA: Association for Supervision and Curriculum Development.

Sousa, D. A. (2001). *How the brain learns: A classroom teacher's guide.* Thousand Oaks, CA: Corwin Press.

Statistics Canada. (2005). Thousands of drop-outs and drop-out rate, Canada and provinces (table). Retrieved June 24, 2010, from http://www.statcan.gc.ca/pub/81-004-x/2005004/8984-eng.htm#table2

Sylwester, R. (1995). *A celebration of neurons: An educator's guide to the human brain.* Alexandria, VA: Association for Supervision and Curriculum Development.

OECD. (2002). *Understanding the brain: Towards a new learning science.* Danvers, MA: Organization for Economic Cooperation and Development. Retrieved June 23, 2010, from http://link.library.utoronto.ca.myaccess. library.utoronto.ca/eir/EIRdetail.cfm?Resources__ ID=217161&T=F

UNESCO. (2007). Global Education Digest 2007. Retrieved June 13, 2010, from http://www.uis.unesco.org/ ev.php?ID=7167_201&ID2=DO_TOPIC

UNESCO, n. d. Education for all. Retrieved June 23, 2010, from website http://stats.uis.unesco.org/unesco/ReportFolders/ ReportFolders.aspx?IF_ActivePath=P,50&IF_ Language=eng

Ungerleider, Ch. (2004). The social determinants of health: Education as a determinant of health. Public Health Agency of Canada. Retrieved Juy 3, 2010, from http://www.phac-aspc.gc.ca/ph-sp/oi-ar/10_education-eng.php

U.S. Department of Education. (2004). Annual secondary education expenditures per student. Retrieved June 15, 2010, from http://www2.ed.gov/about/overview/ fed/10facts/edlite-chart.html

Vygotski, L. S. (1978). In M. Cole (Ed.), *Mind in society: The development of higher psychological processes.* Cambridge, MA: Harvard University Press.

Wolfe, P. (2001). *Brain matters: Translating research into classroom practice.* Alexandra, VA: Association for Supervision and Curriculum Development.